W9-BIP-749

BioCritiques

Maya Angelou
Jane Austen
The Brontë Sisters
Lord Byron
Geoffrey Chaucer
Anton Chekhov
Stephen Crane
Emily Dickinson
William Faulkner
F. Scott Fitzgerald
Robert Frost
Ernest Hemingway
Langston Hughes
Stephen King
Arthur Miller
Toni Morrison
Edgar Allan Poe
J. D. Salinger
William Shakespeare
John Steinbeck
Mark Twain
Alice Walker
Walt Whitman
Tennessee Williams

Bloom's BioCritiques

LANGSTON HUGHES

Edited and with an introduction by
Harold Bloom
Sterling Professor of the Humanities
Yale University

CHELSEA HOUSE PUBLISHERS
Philadelphia

Library of Congress Cataloging-in-Publication Data

Langston Hughes / edited and with an introduction by Harold Bloom.
    p. cm. -- (Bloom's bio critiques)
    Includes bibliographical references and index.
    ISBN 0-7910-6186-8
    1. Hughes, Langston, 1902-1967--Criticism and interpretation. 2. African
    Americans in literature. I. Bloom, Harold. II. Series.

PS3515.U274Z668 2001
818'.5209--dc21

                                                          2001055281

Chelsea House Publishers
1974 Sproul Road, Suite 400
Broomall, PA 19008-0914

http://www.chelseahouse.com

contributing editor: Matt Longabucco

CONTENTS

User's Guide

These volumes are designed to introduce the reader to the life and work of the world's literary masters. Each volume begins with Harold Bloom's essay "The Work in the Writer" and a volume-specific introduction also written by Professor Bloom. Following these unique introductions is an engaging biography that discusses the major life events and important literary accomplishments of the author under consideration.

Furthermore, each volume includes an original critique that not only traces the themes, symbols, and ideas apparent in the author's works, but strives to put those works into a cultural and historical perspectives. In addition to the original critique is a brief selection of significant critical essays previously published on the author and his or her works followed by a concise and informative chronology of the writer's life. Finally, each volume concludes with a bibliography of the writer's works, a list of additional readings, and an index of important themes and ideas.

HAROLD BLOOM

The Work in the Writer

Literary biography found its masterpiece in James Boswell's *Life of Samuel Johnson*. Boswell, when he treated Johnson's writings, implicitly commented upon Johnson as found in his work, even as in the great critic's life. Modern instances of literary biography, such as Richard Ellmann's lives of W. B. Yeats, James Joyce, and Oscar Wilde, essentially follow in Boswell's pattern.

That the writer somehow is in the work, we need not doubt, though with William Shakespeare, writer-of-writers, we almost always need to rely upon pure surmise. The exquisite rancidities of the Problem Plays or Dark Comedies seem to express an extraordinary estrangement of Shakespeare from himself. When we read or attend *Troilus and Cressida* and *Measure for Measure*, we may be startled by particular speeches of Ulysses in the first play, or of Vincentio in the second. These speeches, of Ulysses upon hierarchy or upon time, or of Duke Vincentio upon death, are too strong either for their contexts or for the characters of their speakers. The same phenomenon occurs with Parolles, the military impostor of *All's Well That Ends Well*. Utterly disgraced, he nevertheless affirms: "Simply the thing I am/Shall make me live."

In Shakespeare, more even than in his peers, Dante and Cervantes, meaning always starts itself again through excess or overflow. The strongest of Shakespeare's creatures—Falstaff, Hamlet, Iago, Lear, Cleopatra—have an exuberance that is fiercer than their plays can contain. If Ben Jonson was at all correct in his complaint that "Shakespeare wanted art," it could have been only in a sense that he may not have intended. Where do the personalities of Falstaff or Hamlet touch a limit? What was it in Shakespeare that made the two parts of *Henry IV* and *Hamlet* into "plays unlimited"? Neither Falstaff nor Hamlet will be stopped: their wit, their beautiful, laughing speech, their intensity of being—all these are virtually infinite.

In what ways do Falstaff and Hamlet manifest the writer in the work? Evidently, we can never know, or know enough to answer with any authority. But what would happen if we reversed the question, and asked: How did the work form the writer, Shakespeare?

Of Shakespeare's inwardness, his biography tells us nothing. And yet, to an astonishing extent, Shakespeare created our inwardness. At the least, we can speculate that Shakespeare so lived his life as to conceal the depths of his nature, particularly as he rather prematurely aged. We do not have Shakespeare on Shakespeare, as any good reader of the Sonnets comes to realize: they do not constitute a key that unlocks his heart. No sequence of sonnets could be less confessional or more powerfully detached from the poet's self.

The German poet and universal genius, Goethe, affords a superb contrast to Shakespeare. Of Goethe's life, we know more than everything; I wonder sometimes if we know as much about Napoleon or Freud or any other human being who ever has lived, as we know about Goethe. Everywhere, we can find Goethe in his work, so much so that Goethe seems to crowd the writing out, just as Byron and Oscar Wilde seem to usurp their own literary accomplishments. Goethe, cunning beyond measure, nevertheless invested a rival exuberance in his greatest works that could match his personal charisma. The sublime outrageousness of the Second Part of *Faust*, or of the greater lyric and meditative poems, form a Counter-Sublime to Goethe's own daemonic intensity.

Goethe was fascinated by the daemonic in himself; we can doubt that Shakespeare had any such interests. Evidently, Shakespeare abandoned his acting career just before he composed *Measure for Measure* and *Othello*. I surmise that the egregious interventions by Vincentio and Iago displace the actor's energies into a new kind of mischief-making, a fresh opening to a subtler playwriting-within-the-play.

But what had opened Shakespeare to this new awareness? The answer is the work in the writer, *Hamlet* in Shakespeare. One can go further: it was not so much the play, *Hamlet*, as the character Hamlet, who changed Shakespeare's art forever.

Hamlet's personality is so large and varied that it rivals Goethe's own. Ironically Goethe's Faust, his Hamlet, has no personality at all, and is as colorless as Shakespeare himself seems to have chosen to be. Yet nothing could be more colorful than the Second Part of *Faust*, which is peopled by an astonishing array of monsters, grotesque devils, and classical ghosts.

A contrast between Shakespeare and Goethe demonstrates that in each—but in very different ways—we can better find the work in the person, than we can discover that banal entity, the person in the work. Goethe to many of his contemporaries, seemed to be a mortal god. Shakespeare, so far as we know, seemed an affable, rather ordinary fellow, who aged early and became somewhat withdrawn. Yet Faust, though Mephistopheles battles for his soul, is hardly worth the trouble unless you take him as an idea and not as a person. Hamlet is nearly every-idea-in-one, but he is precisely a personality and a person.

Would Hamlet be so astonishingly persuasive if his father's ghost did not haunt him? Falstaff is more alive than Prince Hal, who says that the devil haunts him in the shape of an old fat man. Three years before composing the final *Hamlet*, Shakespeare invented Falstaff, who then never ceased to haunt his creator. Falstaff and Hamlet may be said to best represent the work in the writer, because their influence upon Shakespeare was prodigious. W.H. Auden accurately observed that Falstaff possesses infinite energy: never tired, never bored, and absolutely both witty and happy until Hal's rejection destroys him. Hamlet too has infinite energy, but in him it is more curse than blessing.

Falstaff and Hamlet can be said to occupy the roles in Shakespeare's invented world that Sancho Panza and Don Quixote possess in Cervantes's. Shakespeare's plays from 1610 on (starting with *Twelfth Night*) are thus analogous to the Second Part of Cervantes's epic novel. Sancho and the Don overtly jostle Cervantes for authorship in the Second Part, even as Cervantes battles against the impostor who has pirated a continuation of his work. As a dramatist, Shakespeare manifests the work in the writer more indirectly. Falstaff's prose genius is revived in the scapegoating of Malvolio by Maria and Sir Toby Belch, while Falstaff's darker insights are developed by Feste's melancholic wit. Hamlet's intellectual resourcefulness, already deadly, becomes poisonous in Iago and in Edmund. Yet we have not crossed into the deeper abysses of the work in the writer in later Shakespeare.

No fictive character, before or since, is Falstaff's equal in self-trust. Sir John, whose delight in himself is contagious, has total confidence both in his self-awareness and in the resources of his language. Hamlet, whose self is as strong, and whose language is as copious, nevertheless distrusts both the self and language. Later Shakespeare is, as it were, much under the influence both of Falstaff and of Hamlet, but they tug him in opposite directions. Shakespeare's own copiousness of language is well-nigh incredible: a vocabulary in excess of twenty-one thousand words, almost eighteen hundred of which he coined himself. And of his word-hoard, nearly half are used only once each, as though the perfect setting for each had been found, and need not be repeated. Love for language and faith in language are Falstaffian attributes. Hamlet will darken both that love and that faith in Shakespeare, and perhaps the Sonnets can best be read as Falstaff and Hamlet counterpointing against one another.

Can we surmise how aware Shakespeare was of Falstaff and Hamlet, once they had played themselves into existence? *Henry IV, Part I* appeared in six quarto editions during Shakespeare's lifetime; *Hamlet* possibly had four. Falstaff and Hamlet were played again and again at the Globe, but Shakespeare knew also that they were being read, and he must have had contact with some of those readers. What would it have been like to discuss Falstaff or Hamlet with one of their early readers (presumably also part of their audience at the Globe), if you were the creator of such demiurges? The question would seem nonsensical to most Shakespeare scholars, but then these days they tend to be either ideologues or moldy figs. How can we recover the uncanniness of Falstaff and of Hamlet, when they now have become so familiar?

A writer's influence upon himself is an unexplored problem in criticism, but such an influence is never free from anxieties. The biocritical problem (which this series attempts to explore) can be divided into two areas, difficult to disengage fully. Accomplished works affect the author's life, and also affect her subsequent writings. It is simpler for me to surmise the effect of *Mrs. Dalloway* and *To the Lighthouse* upon Woolf's late *Between the Acts*, than it is to relate Clarissa Dalloway's suicide and Lily Briscoe's capable endurance in art to the tragic death and complex life of Virginia Woolf.

There are writers whose lives were so vivid that they seem sometimes to obscure the literary achievement: Byron, Wilde, Malraux, Hemingway. But most major Western writers do not live that exuberantly, and the greatest of all, Shakespeare, sometimes appears to have adopted the personal mask of colorlessness. And yet there are heroes of literature who struggled titanically with their own eras—Tolstoy, Milton, Victor Hugo—who nevertheless matter more for their works than their lives.

There are great figures—Emily Dickinson, Wallace Stevens, Willa Cather—who seem to have had so little of the full intensity of life when compared to the vitality of their work, that we might almost speak of the work in the work, rather than even of the work in a person. Emily Brontë might well be the extreme instance of such a visionary, surpassing William Blake in that one regard.

I conclude this general introduction to a series of literary bio-critiques by stating a tentative formula or principle for gauging the many ways in which the work influences the person and her subsequent, later work. Our influence upon ourselves is always related to the Shakespearean invention of self-overhearing, which I have written about in several other contexts. Life, as well as poetry and prose, is overheard rather than simply heard. The writer listens to herself as though she were somebody else, and the will to change begins to operate. The forces that live in us include the prior work we have done, and the dreams and waking visions that evade our dismissals.

HAROLD BLOOM

Introduction

Langston Hughes, despite the public aspects of his career, lived and died essentially in solitude. Much of his early life was spent yearning for his mother, a beautiful would-be actress who manifested little affection for her only child. His maternal grandmother, Mary Langston, raised him to the family tradition of rebellion on behalf of African-American rights. Her first husband was killed, fighting by John Brown's side, at Harper's Ferry in 1859, while her second—Langston Hughes's grandfather—helped organize the black regiments in the Union Army. Hughes, partly in consequence, associated himself with the Communist Party, though in testimony before Senator Joseph McCarthy's notorious committee he denied membership. Unfortunately, he cooperated with McCarthy, and alienated permanently a number of good acquaintances, including W.E.B. Du Bois and Paul Robeson. More and more isolated, his sexual impulses repressed, Hughes became a voice for his people, but at the cost of vital elements in his personal self.

Hughes's two autobiographies—*The Big Sea* (1940) and *I Wonder as I Wander* (1956), remain very readable, as do his short stories. His plays are more problematic, but his permanent fame as a populist poet, in what he took to be the tradition of Carl Sandburg and Paul Laurence Dunbar is assured. A sophisticated literary consciousness who deliberately schooled himself to work in the modes of the blues, spirituals, and varied jazz forms, Hughes risked the dangers of over-simplification, since his lines on the page have to carry their own internal music. An exemplary chant like "Let

1

America Be America Again" is poignant yet verbally inadequate to meet the immense demands for eloquence that it requires.

Arnold Rampersad, author of the superb *The Life of Langston Hughes* (two volumes, 1986 an 1988), confirms Hughes's own analysis that "my best poems were all written when I felt the worst." His augmenting isolation, despite his literary fame, seems to inform his better poems, some of which are epigrams, such as "Tower":

> Death is a tower
> To which the soul ascends
> To spend a meditative hour—
> That never ends.

That is like a fragment by Emily Dickinson, and testifies to Hughes's unbelief, as he was not a Christian, despite his cultural fondness for African American spirituals and spirituality. And yet there is an unknown element in Hughes's poetry, which fascinates me, though I could not persuade the late Ralph Ellison—who did not care for Hughes's work—to be interested in it. Hughes read widely, but I find no trace even in Rampersad's exhaustive researches of any awareness on Hughes's part of esoteric or heretical strains in American religion, whatever its racial context. And yet Hughes, in his solitude, might be termed a natural gnostic, somehow knowing that what was best and oldest in him was no part either of nature or of history. His hidden homoeroticism, which pragmatically allied him to Walt Whitman, perhaps augmented his sense of spiritual autonomy, which emerges in some of his most famous poems in ways that criticism, being primarily concerned with sociopolitical matters, is very tardy in recognizing.

Hughes's best-known poem always may be "The Negro Speaks of Rivers," which makes a superb contrast to Hart Crane's "Repose of Rivers." In both poems the poet and the river or rivers fuse, almost into a single voice. Crane's poem concerns the process of poetic incarnation, which is identified also with the recognition of homoerotic orientation. Hughes, always evasive, speaks of "knowing" rivers—ancient, dusky, and profound as the black soul—but they are "older than the flow of human blood in human veins." Why does Hughes risk the (only) apparent redundancy of repeating the word "human"? The origin evidently is set before our present condition, of whatever race or mixture we are (Hughes's own ancestry included French, African, and Native American strains). This hints at a Hermetic or Gnostic myth (first suggested to me by the late Kenneth Burke in conversation). Hughes's sensibility was thwarted both religiously and sexually, and that allied frustration breaks through in this curiously primordial poem. How ought we to interpret the final line: "My soul has grown deep like the rivers?"

We should be wary of sounding the soul's depths, particularly with a soul as isolated as that of Langston Hughes, an outsider's outsider, who by paradox because one of the voice of the people with whom he chose to identify. Under-reading is the curse of Hughes-criticism. "The Negro Speaks of Rivers" assumes the accent of authority, and justifies it. I hear in the poem a knowing so sophisticated that it becomes esoteric and heretical, whatever its overt intentionality.

Something like this appears again in the fierce "Song for a Dark Girl" where Christianity is rejected: "I asked the white Lord Jesus/ What was the use of prayer." At the poem's close, Hughes achieves a memorable intensity: "Love is a naked shadow/ On a gnarled and naked tree." This is a lynching and a crucifixion, but the cross may be naked also. The Gnostics maintained that only a shadow, and not the man Jesus, expired upon the cross. Hughes again intimates what he explicitly might now have intended, but the shadow adds complexity to the plangency of his lament.

CINDY DYSON

Biography of Langston Hughes

LOST CHILD

An 18-year-old boy, who just finished high school, looked out the train window as the sun set over the Mississippi River. Tension jabbed at his stomach. He had left his mother in Cleveland and was on his way to Mexico to visit a father he didn't like. He was black, poor, and full of dreams that were not likely to come true.

As he watched the sun dance off the river, turning its muddy waters gold and orange, he fished in his pocket for a scrap of paper. Langston Hughes began to write:

> I've known rivers:
> I've known rivers ancient as the world and older
> than the flow of human blood in human veins.
> My soul has grown deep like the rivers.
> I bathed in the Euphrates when the dawns were
> young.
> I built my hut near the Congo and it lulled me to
> sleep.
> I looked upon the Nile and raised the pyramids
> above it.
> I heard the singing of the Mississippi when Abe
> Lincoln went down to New Orleans, and I've seen

its muddy bosom turn all golden in the sunset.
I've known rivers:
Ancient, dusky rivers.
   My soul has grown deep like rivers.

Hughes had two dreams that evening in 1920—he wanted to go to college and he wanted to be a writer. The poem, "The Negro Speaks of Rivers," would become one of his most famous. It spoke of the themes Hughes would continue to revisit throughout much of his writing career—racial pride and endurance.

Langston's father James had left the family for Mexico in hopes of escaping the racism and segregation that plagued the United States. Hughes recalled his father as being a man who had little tolerance for the poor, especially poor blacks—often sneering at them and calling them niggers.

All day on the train I had been thinking about my father and his strange dislike of his own people, [Hughes remembered]. I didn't understand it, because I was a Negro, and I liked Negroes very much. . . . They seemed to me like the gayest and the bravest people possible—these Negroes from the Southern ghettos— facing tremendous odds, working and laughing and trying to get somewhere in the world.

James's invitation came at a critical juncture in young Langston's life. He was about to graduate from high school and sought the means by which he could attend college. His father had done well financially and seemed to be Langston's best hope at financing his education.

"He hinted that he would send me to college if I intended to go, and he thought I had better go," Langston remembered.

"I didn't want to return to Mexico, but I had a feeling I'd never get any further education if I didn't, since my mother wanted me to go to work and be, as she put it, 'of some use to her.'"

As Langston settled in, he realized that his father was willing, even eager, to pay for his education—if he agreed to study mining engineering, a profession James felt would secure his son's future. Langston refused. He tried to explain that he wanted to be a writer and to write about black people.

"A writer?" James said. "A writer? Do they make any money?"

"Some of them do, I guess."

"I never heard of a colored one that did. . . . Learn something you can make a living from anywhere in the world, in Europe or South America, and don't stay in the States, where you have to live like a nigger with niggers."

"But I like Negroes," Langston said. "We have plenty of fun."

"Fun! How can you have fun with the color line staring you in the face? I never could."

When his father questioned why he would want to write about black people and live in an America that despised and mistreated blacks, Langston replied, "I love them. That is where I want to be and that is where I will stay."

Langston knew it would take a concerted effort to change his father's mind.

He spent his days learning Spanish, teaching English classes, and, because his father had arranged it, studying at a business college. Socially, Hughes became part of an elite circle of friends. With his good looks, easygoing manner, and his father's standing in the community, he was soon invited to many of the best social events and outings and to bullfights in Mexico City.

During this time, Hughes was also writing. In September he sent three articles and a play to *Brownies' Book*, a magazine for black children. Editor Jessie Fauset accepted them. She also asked if he had any original Mexican stories and Mexican children's games he could send. He quickly sent an article on games and several poems. The January issue contained two of Hughes's poems, his first exposure in a national magazine.

That month Hughes decided to aim higher, and he sent "The Negro Speaks of Rivers" to *The Crisis*, the official magazine of the National Association for the Advancement of Colored People. Fauset and W.E.B. Du Bois, who had helped found the N.A.A.C.P, edited the magazine. Fauset accepted the poem immediately. Suddenly she had this mysterious new talent, a young black man in Mexico, sending her beautiful work month after month.

In her correspondence with Hughes she wrote, "May I be a bit curious? You write so well and sympathetically—who are you, and whence and why do you live in Mexico?"

In June of 1921, "The Negro Speaks of Rivers" was published in *The Crisis*. One month later the influential and nationally recognized journal *Literary Digest* reprinted the poem. Fauset and Du Bois were excited about this new talent they'd discovered. That summer they devoted an entire page to Hughes's poetry. At nineteen, he'd become a regular in the most important journal in black America.

"With the timidity of a child but the guile of an ancient," wrote biographer Arnold Rampersad, "Langston had begun his seduction of Harlem." In the next few months, he was widely published in *Brownies'* and *The Crisis*. His father grudgingly agreed to pay for a year of college at Columbia University, and in September 1921, Langston set off for New York.

Eventually dubbed the "Shakespeare of Harlem," Hughes published sixteen volumes of poetry, ten collections of short stories, two novels, two autobiographies, nine books for children, more than two dozen stage works, along with numerous articles, films, radio scripts, song lyrics, anthologies, and translations. Furthermore Hughes established black theater groups while traveling and lecturing around the world. He became the most famous and well-read black poet of his time and helped to change the landscape for black artists in America.

In his lifetime, however, Langston Hughes never achieved the success he envisioned when he set off for New York. He never had a best-seller or a Broadway hit. While he remained poor most of his life, he lived generously, giving away his talents whenever he thought they were needed. In his own words, he was a "literary sharecropper," eking out a living as a writer while depending on the good will of others.

He was essentially lonely yet made thousands of friends; he was a nomad who longed for a home. He was part of an elite circle of intellectuals, but spent his days and nights in the poorest neighborhoods carousing in the more unsavory parts of towns. Hughes firmly believed that his words could change lives. He was never just a writer, he was a black writer.

HERO HERITAGE

Langston's mother, Carrie Langston, and his father, James Hughes, met around 1898 when Carrie moved to Guthrie in the Oklahoma Territory. There, the stylish, talented young woman, who had always wanted a career on the stage, settled for a teaching job. It was also here in Guthrie that Carrie caught the eye of the town's most ambitious black man— a teacher, law clerk, and homesteader named James Hughes. James was the descendent of two prominent white grandfathers from Kentucky.

The two were married on April 30, 1899, and within days Carrie became pregnant. Always aspiring to something more than scraping a living off the land, James and his wife moved to Joplin, Missouri, where James got a job as a stenographer. Here in Joplin, the couple briefly settled into a house in a respectable neighborhood. Shortly thereafter, Carrie lost that first child, and the couple was once again on the move. From Joplin, they moved to Buffalo, New York, with further plans to move to Cuba. James believed black people had a better chance of success in Cuba, but the move was abandoned when once again Carrie learned she was pregnant. Instead of Cuba, Carrie went back to Joplin, where Langston was born on February 1, 1902. James had considered going with her, but, unwilling to suffer the consequences of segregation in the United States, he quickly left for Mexico.

When Langston was five, he and his mother traveled to Mexico to join James. Shortly afterwards, a devastating earthquake hit Mexico on April 14, 1907, in which hundreds died. Langston remembered his father carrying him out to the street, where he saw crowds kneeling in prayer. The chaos and death were too much for Carrie. She took Langston and returned to the states.

Carrie realized she couldn't take care of Langston alone and left him with her mother, Mary Langston, in Lawrence, Kansas. The time Langston spent with his grandmother would profoundly influence his ideas of what it meant to be black in America.

Mary was in her seventies when Langston came to her. She owned a two-bedroom home near the University of Kansas in a mostly white section of town. Mary was born free, but an attempt to enslave her forced her to go to the abolitionist stronghold of Ohio. Her first husband, Lewis Sheridan Leary, was one of the 18 men who fought beside John Brown in 1859 during his famous raid at Harper's Ferry—now West Virginia—to free slaves. Ten of Brown's men were killed there and Lewis was one of them. Mary kept the bullet-ridden shawl he wore when he died.

Ten years later Mary married another abolitionist, Charles Howard Langston, the son of a rich white Virginian planter and a former slave with both Indian and African blood. Charles became the first black person to attend Oberlin College and was active in politics, black newspaper publishing, and recruiting blacks for the Civil War. Charles's brother John Langston, also an abolitionist, served as a congressman for the state of Virginia.

Wrapping her late husband's shawl around little Langston, Mary often pulled him onto her lap and told him all these stories. She talked of how she had been the first black woman to attend Oberlin College and further told him how his father had studied law. Langston understood, even as a boy, that he had a proud heritage and a duty to live up to it.

After several months with his grandmother, Carrie reappeared, determined to take care of Langston herself. The two moved to Topeka, Kansas, where Carrie had a job. It was also in Topeka where Langston first experienced the pangs of segregation as Carrie tried to enroll him in first grade at the nearby Harrison Street School. Eli S. Foster, the principal at Harrison, insisted that Langston attend the Washington School for colored children some distance away. Carrie stood firm, arguing that Langston was too young to walk the distance alone. Further refused, Carrie took her case to the school board and won. Almost 50 years later, the landmark Supreme Court decision against the same school board, Topeka Board of Education, would officially end segregation in the United States.

Unfortunately, Carrie's victory was only the first such instance when Langston was exposed to discrimination. On the first day of class, the teacher seated everyone alphabetically—except him. He sat in the last row, in the corner of the room. Later in the year, his teacher had snatched licorice sticks away from a white child saying, "You don't want to eat these," and, "they'll make you black like Langston. You don't want to be black, do you?"

Before the school year was over, Carrie had pulled Langston out of Harrison and deposited him back at his grandmother's. He started second grade at the Pinckney School with other black children, and for the first time, he had a black teacher. The school's first three grades were segregated, and integrated beginning with the fourth grade. Eighty years later the school's library would be named after Langston Hughes.

Langston did well at Pinckney. He had black and white friends and often impressed his teachers. Mary kept a tight rein on him and insisted he come right home after school. However, her insistence proved unnecessary as blacks were not allowed to participate in after-school activities such as swimming at the local YMCA, joining the Boy Scouts, or participating in school sports.

Throughout much of the country, particularly in the South, racist attitudes were institutionalized with what were known as Jim Crow laws, segregating and barring black people from public places and many jobs. It wasn't just schools that separated blacks and whites. Restrooms, drinking fountains, theaters, trains, buses, restaurants, and hotels were either off-limits to black people or were segregated. Jim Crow was a way of life for Hughes, but that didn't mean he accepted it easily.

In eighth grade, his white teacher segregated her classroom, putting her few black students in a separate row. In defiance, Hughes propped up cards on the desks, labeling the seats the Jim Crow Row. When the teacher tried to stop him, Hughes ran into the schoolyard, yelling that his teacher had a Jim Crow row. He was promptly expelled. Fortunately, Carrie was in town and took his case to the school administrators, who reinstated Langston and forced the teacher to drop her segregated seating.

Throughout his grammar school days, Carrie made occasional visits during which she would whisk Langston away for a trip or take him to the theater or a concert. He longed for his mother and waited anxiously for her next return, but she would never be the kind of mother Langston needed. Carrie's efforts were focused more on buying clothes, traveling, and trying to build a career on stage than being a mother. At times, he felt that she blamed him for her failure to make it as an actress or for not making enough money.

"You're just like Jim Hughes," she would snap at Langston. "You're as evil as Jim Hughes." Langston withdrew from such criticism, further angering his mother. She began calling him "dull" and "stupid." As Hughes got older, some of his hurt turned to anger. On one such occasion when Carrie arrived in town to present a play at a local church, Langston retaliated. He and another boy were supposed to stand on stage, wrapped in togas, while Carrie recited a monologue. As she began to speak, he grimaced and the audience tittered. As Carrie's voice rose to cover the chuckles, Langston made more faces. The audience burst out laughing, ruining Carrie's scene. She was furious and gave him a whipping.

Gradually, Hughes's feelings of rejection grew. He developed a deeper fantasy life, away from his irresponsible mother and strict grandmother. Hughes had discovered the library.

> The silence inside the library, the big chairs, and long tables, and the fact that the library was always there and didn't seem to have a mortgage on it, or any sort of insecurity about it—all of that made me love it. And right then, . . . books began to happen to me, so that after a while, there came a time when I believed in books more than in people—which, of course, was wrong.

At the library, he read W.E.B. Du Bois, the Bible, the poems of black poet Paul Laurence Dunbar, Zane Grey novels, *Uncle Tom's Cabin*, and *The Adventures of Huckleberry Finn*. He also read the *Chicago Defender*, a weekly black newspaper that told stories of lynchings and called for black people to fight racism.

In 1915, when Langston was just 13, his grandmother died in the night. He didn't cry; she had taught him otherwise. "Nobody ever cried in my grandmother's stories," he remembered. "They worked, or schemed, or fought. But no crying. When my grandmother died, I didn't cry, either. Something about my grandmother's stories (without her ever having said so) taught me the uselessness of crying about anything."

Once again, Hughes was adrift. He longed for a family to love and accept him, but he wouldn't find that love in his own family. As critic and biographer Arnold Rampersad notes, as a teen Hughes began looking to black culture for the acceptance he craved:

> Already he had begun to identify not his family but the poorest and most despised blacks as the object of his ultimate desire to please. He would need the race, and would need to appease the race, to an extent felt by few other blacks, and by no other important black writer . . . it originated in an equally rare combination of a sense of racial destiny with a keen knowledge of childhood hurt.

THE ROAD TO HARLEM

Hughes's only solace in his grandmother's death was that it might reunite him with his mother and her new family. During Langston's time with Mary, his mother had married Homer Clark and together they had a son, Gwyn. Hughes was crushed when his mother pawned him off on friends the summer after Mary's death. Again, he had been abandoned. He turned his hopes for a family toward his father. He dreamed about his father as "a kind of strong, bronze cowboy, in a big Mexican hat, going back and forth from his business in the city to his ranch in the mountains free [in] the mountains and sun and cacti: Mexico!"

Late in the summer of his 13th year, his mother asked him to move to Lincoln, Illinois, where she, Homer, and Gwyn had settled. Langston rode the train alone to the small town.

He started eighth grade at the Lincoln Central School. The school was integrated, but Hughes and another girl were the only blacks. He was well liked at school. His teachers found him bright and oddly mature. Students thought he was friendly and good-looking. They elected him class poet. Hughes would say later that they picked him because they assumed, as a black person, he had a better sense of rhythm than the white students. As class poet, he was expected to read a poem he'd written for grammar school graduation.

"In the first half of the poem, I said that our school had the finest teachers there ever were," Hughes recalled. "And in the latter half, I said our class was the greatest class ever graduated. Naturally everybody applauded loudly. That was the way I began to write poetry."

By the end of the next summer, Langston's family was on the move again. Homer found work as a machinist at a steel mill in Cleveland, Ohio. World War I was in full swing. Black people were flocking to manufacturing cities like Cleveland to snap up the jobs opening up to them as white workers enlisted.

Hughes loved Cleveland; it was the first big city he had lived in. Although the family lived in a cramped basement apartment, Hughes's lifelong passion for cities began here. He marveled at the mansions, the shops, ornate buildings, theaters, and music halls.

The following year at Central High School began much as one would expect—Hughes again earned good grades, made friends, and had a family to come home to everyday. This stability didn't last. Homer wasn't able to keep his steel mill job and left to find work in Chicago. After several weeks, Carrie took Gwyn and went after him, leaving Langston to fend for himself.

Hughes rented an attic room and tried to take care of himself. The only things he knew how to cook were rice and hot dogs, which he ate nearly every night. Fortunately, he met a couple who had just started a community service center called the Playground House. Russell and Rowena Jelliffe, a white couple interested in helping the struggling blacks around them, invited him into their book-filled home. Hughes spent many evenings there, reading and dozing, before returning to his room alone.

As he read, he began to think about writing stories himself:

> I never will forget the thrill of first understanding the French of de Maupassant, [Hughes recalled]. The soft snow was falling through one of his stories in the little book we used in school, and that I had worked over so long, before I really felt the snow falling there. Then all of a sudden one night the beauty and the meaning of the words in which he made the snow fall, came to me. I think it was de Maupassant who made me really want to be a writer and write stories about Negroes, so true that people in faraway lands would read them—even after I was dead.

In the fall of 1918, Langston began his junior year. He joined the staff of the school magazine and began contributing regularly. Four of his poems appeared in the first issue. In December he published his first short story. In January, two of his poems and another short story appeared. He began his lifelong habit of writing poems on scraps of paper when they came to him. When he had time, he'd transfer them to a notebook.

His work was getting better. An English teacher had introduced him to poets Walt Whitman, Vachel Lindsay, and Carl Sandburg, whom Hughes would call his "guiding star." These poets had revolutionized poetry, stripping it of its measured meter, studied rhyme, and lofty themes. Hughes began to follow their lead into free verse and poems for and about ordinary people. He began sending his poems to magazines. But each one came back with a curt rejection note.

Central High School was a cosmopolitan place, where Langston fit right in. He was elected to the student council, excelled in track and field, and belonged to the home garden club and the French club.

But outside the school's walls, racism prevailed. Once, when his French class attended a performance, Langston and a white friend went into a cafeteria. The cashier continued ringing items into the register until his bill totaled $8.65. His friend had a similar amount of food and paid about .50 cents.

"Why is mine so much?" Langston asked.

"That is just what you will pay if you eat here," the cashier said.

"But I don't have that much food."

"That is what you will pay to eat it," the cashier snipped.

Langston left his tray in front of her and went to where his friend had already taken a seat. "Come on, let's get out of here. They won't let me eat in this place."

During the last half of his junior year, his mother and Gwyn returned to Cleveland. Homer had left them again.

That spring, Langston's father reentered his life. He sent $60 and a note announcing he would be stopping by in Cleveland after a trip to New York. He wanted to take Langston back to Mexico for the summer. Langston was ecstatic. Finally, his father, that independent cowboy he had idolized, was coming to his rescue. Carrie, however, was outraged. She called Langston disloyal and ungrateful for wanting to see his father.

The family had moved and James's telegram announcing that he was coming on the night train didn't get to Langston until the next morning. Fearing his father had left without him, Langston called hotels until he found a James Hughes listed. Rushing to the hotel, his eyes scanned the street for a man who could be his father. When he saw James, a bronze man with a bushy mustache and cropped hair, walking toward him on the street, he passed right by. James looked back. "Are you Langston?" he asked.

"Yes," Langston replied. "Are you my father?"

"Why weren't you at the train last night?"

"We moved, and I didn't get your wire till this morning."

"Just like niggers. Always moving!"

And so began the dissolution of his fantasy father. The father who would love, accept, and ease Langston's loneliness was replaced by a hurried, intolerant man.

James Hughes had done well in Mexico. With his light skin, fluency in Spanish and English, and his knowledge of both American and Mexican law, he had amassed more wealth than anyone else in the Hughes Family. He owned property in Mexico City, a big ranch in Temexcaltepic, and a house in Toluca, where he brought Langston.

Soon after he arrived, Langston realized that his father wanted more than a visit. He wanted to train him to take over his business affairs and began teaching him bookkeeping skills. As Hughes recalls:

> I was never very good at figures, and I got hopelessly tangled up in the problems he gave me. My stupidity disgusted him immeasurably, and he would rail at me about the need of acquiring a good business head. Seventeen and you can't add yet!

Then he would bend over the ledger and show me all over again how to balance the spoiled page, and say: Now, hurry up and do it! Hurry up! Hurry up!

James's attitude toward other blacks and poor Mexicans also hardened Langston against his father. Hughes watched his father treat the housekeeper and servants with obvious contempt. An Indian boy employed by his father slept on a pile of sacks in a tool shed and wasn't allowed to eat inside the house.

During his stay, Hughes occupied his time by befriending a servant who taught him to ride bareback, learning to cook Mexican dishes, and shooting his father's pistols. However, none of this erased his boredom, depression, or disillusionment with his father. So desperate were the times that he one day went so far as to put a loaded pistol to his head. Thinking of all he would miss, Langston Hughes put the gun down.

The depression didn't end. Hughes came down with a high fever and James took him to a hospital in Mexico City, where he was diagnosed with a stomach virus. He later said that the real reason for his illness had a lot to do with his anger toward his father. He remained at the hospital for several weeks. This would not be the last time Hughes's tendency to keep his anger bottled up would make him ill.

Hughes rode the train back to Cleveland in September 1919, eager to escape his father. He settled in with his mother to finish high school. He got an after-school job in a hotel dining room, became an officer in the school's drill corps, lettered in track and field, acted in plays, remained in the French club, and edited the school yearbook.

In the spring of 1920, he wrote the first poem that foreshadowed his coming career. The poem, "When Susanna Jones Wears Red," praised the beauty of a black girl he knew, drawing on the rhythms of black speech. He had seen his father turn away from his race; Langston meant to embrace it. When he was again named class poet and asked to read a poem at his June 16, 1920, commencement, he had earned the title.

More than anything else, Langston Hughes wanted to go to college. But he had no money. So when his father invited him to Mexico again after graduation, Langston agreed. He wasn't eager to reenter James Hughes's world, but neither did he want to stay in Cleveland working in hotels.

His time in Mexico didn't draw him any closer to his father, but James eventually agreed to pay for a year at Columbia University in New York. In September 1921, Langston said good-bye to his father for the last time and headed for New York.

Columbia University, with its proximity to Harlem and history of academic excellence, held great appeal to Hughes. In 1921, Harlem was in the midst of its greatest period, which came to be known as the Harlem Renaissance. Starting in 1905, when black tenants were allowed to move into the area near Fifth Avenue and 134th Street in the Harlem District, the area became a Mecca for blacks seeking prosperity in one of the most influential cities of the world. Soon the most important black magazines and organizations were headquartered in Harlem. Theaters in Manhattan were opening up to black musicians and actors, drawing black writers and the growing black intelligentsia. As Hughes recalled:

> It was a period when local and visiting royalty were not at all uncommon in Harlem. . . . It was a period when Harold Jackman, a handsome young Harlem school teacher of modest means, calmly announced one day that he was sailing for the Riviera for a fortnight, to attend Princess Murats' yachting party. . . . It was a period when at least one charming colored chorus girl, amber enough to pass for a Latin American, was living in a pent house, with all her bills paid by a gentleman whose name was banker's magic on Wall Street. . . . And when books by Negro authors were being published with much greater frequency and much more publicity than ever before or since in history. . . . It was the period when the Negro was in Vogue. I was there. I had a swell time while it lasted.

As soon as he arrived in New York, Hughes headed for the Harlem branch of the YMCA, dropped his bags in his room, and turned around and headed out to explore "the greatest Negro city in the world."

A WORLD TO SEE

Columbia was a monument of granite and red brick that barred blacks from the university dorms. When Hughes tried to get a room, he was told they were all taken. He gave proof of his reservation and because his application had come from Mexico, and because he hadn't listed his race on the application form, Hughes was finally given a room.

Despite his hunger to attend college, Hughes found Columbia less than exciting. During his first semester there, Carrie and Gwyn came to New York, eager to take advantage of his new home in the glamorous city. Langston had to find a place for them to live and support them until his mother could find work. Before long, Hughes fell behind in his studies and his money drained away, as Hughes spent much of his time going to shows, concerts, and lectures.

Meanwhile, Fauset from *The Crisis* learned that her mysterious writer from Mexico was in town, and she invited him to meet with her and Du Bois. Both prominent black thinkers were immediately taken with Hughes and introduced him to other prominent black people in the city. He was able to publish more poems in *The Crisis* and a few other journals and magazines.

By the end of the spring semester Hughes had barely passed his courses and showed little interest in continuing his studies at Columbia. Instead, he wanted to see the world.

Eager to travel but with no money, he looked for a job on a ship. Blacks were rarely hired, and when they were, the only job typically open to them was mess boy—cleaning sailors' quarters, clothes, and galleys. Walking the New York docks, Hughes was surprised when he was offered a job. He was so excited that he didn't think to ask where the ship was going. He packed a few things and boarded. However, instead of going out to sea, the ship traveled up the Hudson River. It was a support ship for a mothballed fleet of poorly built warships that had been towed up the Hudson and anchored just in case they were needed. Hughes's job was to clean up after the skeleton crew of sailors watching over the fleet.

He loved playing cards and singing with the sailors and listening to their stories of places like Bombay and Cape Town. He remained on the ship through a long, lonely winter, listening to the wind howling and the creaking chains as the ships strained at anchor. The unique combination of camaraderie and isolation during Hughes's experience on board inspired an intensely creative period. He began experimenting with capturing the sound of blues music in poetry and wrote two celebrated poems that year, "The Weary Blues" and "Mother to Son," rich with images of loneliness and a love for black culture.

During that long winter of 1922, an eminent black professor at Howard University began writing to Hughes. Alain Locke had read some of Hughes's poems and was taken with him. Hughes's most prominent biographer, Rampersad, asserted that Alain was romantically interested in Hughes. Whether or not Hughes was aware of Alain's sexual interest is unknown. He wrote back to Alain, not wanting to alienate an important black intellectual, keeping his letters somewhat aloof.

By that spring, Hughes had decided to find a ship that was actually going somewhere. Again he plied the docks, and in June 1923 he found a spot on the S.S. Malone headed for the west coast of Africa. It would be a hot, rainy, malarial trip, and it was difficult to get a crew.

For American blacks, Africa was in vogue at the time. The back-to-Africa movement was in full swing in 1923, with prominent blacks calling for a return to their homelands. Blacks were becoming interested and vocal about fighting against the colonialism that gripped much of Africa. W.E.B. Du Bois himself had helped create the Pan-African Congress, which railed against European colonization of black Africa. However, most of these American blacks had never been there. At age 21, Hughes was on his way.

As the ship headed out to sea, Hughes felt he was being set free. He was leaving his old self, all his loneliness and uncertainty behind. He was heading for fabled Africa, home of his ancestors and the brothers and sisters of his race. Suddenly, he felt compelled to separate himself from his past. He had brought a box of books to read on the journey, but now he dragged them onto the deck and tossed them overboard—all but one—Walt Whitman's seminal book of poetry, *Leaves of Grass*. Hughes later wrote of this experience:

> It was like throwing a million bricks out of my heart—for it wasn't only the books that I wanted to throw away, but every thing unpleasant and miserable out of my past: the memory of my father, the poverty and uncertainties of my mother's life, the stupidities of color-prejudice, black in a white world, the fear of not finding a job, the bewilderment of no one to talk to about things that trouble you, the feeling of always being controlled by others—by parents, by employers, by some outer necessity not your own. All those things I wanted to throw away.

Unsurprisingly, Africa was not what Hughes had expected. He expected to feel a kinship with other black people—to feel at home. At Port Harcourt, Nigeria, he met a mulatto boy whose English father had abandoned him. The boy told how Africans shunned him because of his light skin. Is it true, he asked, that in America black people are friendly to mulattoes?

The question startled Hughes. In America a person with just one black ancestor was considered black. Here only people with all black ancestors were considered black. To his astonishment, black Africans considered him a white man. When he insisted he was black, they often thought he was mocking them. Hughes wrote about these shades of color and racism in two poems, "Brothers" and "Poem."

As Hughes's ship journeyed 90 miles up the Belgian Congo, into what would become the first independent African nation of Ghana 40 years later, he saw the stark realities of what colonialism had done to Africans. The towns were economically depressed and entirely dependent on plantations, where overseers with whips controlled the black workers, and armed black soldiers patrolled the docks. He saw poverty and squalor, but he also saw beauty, strength, and pride in the land and the people. Hughes absorbed Africa—the colors and rhythms of its coastal dunes and the dense misty jungles. When the ship set off for New York, Hughes returned with two things: a better understanding of the complexities of race and Africa's colonial rule, and a big red monkey, named Jocko, for Gwyn.

He stopped in Pittsburgh, where Carrie and Gwyn now lived, to give the monkey to Gwyn. Gwyn loved Jocko, but Carrie couldn't stand the way he pulled on her apron strings and stole her sewing thimbles. As soon as Hughes returned to New York, she sold Jocko.

Still broke and uncertain about his future, Hughes looked for another ship job. In February 1924, he was hired on a ship going to Rotterdam, England, then to Holland. It was a dismal trip. He clashed with another crewmember, found little time to write, and was confused about his future. When the crew was given shore leave in Rotterdam, he jumped ship and immediately bought a ticket on the night train to Paris. The city pulsed with the jazz music brought over by American blacks that consumed upper class Parisians. Hughes found a job at an upscale jazz club where famous authors and royalty often dropped in. He fell in love with jazz, which drew from the blues but added complexity and spontaneity. He often sat at his garret room window overlooking the red tile rooftops of Paris and tried to incorporate the music into his poems, which he continued sending to *The Crisis* and other journals.

At this time, Hughes also became involved with a woman named Anne Marie Coussey. Anne Marie came from an upper class British family. She was brown-skinned, well-read, well-off —and engaged. But Anne Marie wasn't excited about the Englishman her father had arranged for her to marry. She'd read some of Hughes's poems in *The Crisis* and was enchanted by his cultured, yet adventurous, character. He was a handsome man. Just under five foot five, with a slim build. He exuded elegance and poise, tinged with just enough Bohemian to be exciting.

Hughes spent many afternoons in front of Anne Marie's fireplace, sipping tea and talking. She had fallen for Hughes, but didn't know how serious he was about her. Despite what feeling Hughes may have had for Anne Marie, he worried that marriage would force him to put aside his writing in favor of a more financially secure career. By late spring, when he still hadn't proposed, Anne Marie headed back to England and their relationship ended.

Before long, however, Alain Locke showed up in Paris. He and Hughes had been corresponding for the past year-and-a-half and now they explored Paris together. Alain introduced Hughes to the better parts of the city and to its well-known artists. That summer they set off for a tour of Italy.

When their trip came to an end, he and Alain took a train to Genoa, Italy, to catch a boat back to America. On the train, Hughes's passport and wallet were stolen. He had neither the money nor the papers necessary to book passage. Alain left Hughes a bit of money and went on without him. The best way to get home, Hughes figured, was to get a job on a ship headed for New York. He prowled the docks but none of the ships were hiring blacks. Broke and desperate, he fell in with a group of equally desperate Americans and a Scotsman. The group lived by their wits, tricking tourists out of money, stealing food, and keeping a lookout for the police.

He watched white sailors snatch up jobs while he stayed behind, broke and tired. One day he sat in a park, seething with anger, and wrote a poem derived from one of Walt Whitman's most famous celebratory American poems:

> I, too, sing America
>
> I am the darker brother.
> They send me
> To eat in the kitchen
> When company comes,
> But I laugh.
> And eat well,
> And grow strong. . .

At last, in October, after a desperate month in Genoa, Hughes got a job on a ship with an all-black crew. He chipped and painted his way back across the Atlantic.

Upon his arrival in New York Hughes was quick to discover that he had become a celebrated Harlem poet. He was immediately swept into an elite circle of black artists and writers—quite a contrast to the poverty he had only just experienced.

On the evening he returned, Hughes attended a benefit cabaret sponsored by the N.A.A.C.P. As he stepped into the nightclub, he was given a table of honor and introduced to Carl Van Vechten, a leading white music critic and popular novelist who would champion Hughes's work to white publishers in the years to come. A few days later, friends hosted a party honoring Hughes. All of Harlem's elite showed up. As Rampersad notes:

> Hughes did not seem to understand the powerful impact he had made with certain poems in the Crisis. Asked about his latest work, he modestly pulled scraps from his pocket and opened a

tattered notebook, then riveted the audience with a masterful reading. The months in Africa and Europe had been to some purpose.

It wasn't just his work that made Hughes a hit in Harlem, it was the man himself. He was self-deprecating, yet exciting, loyal, sincere, and fun.

If I had to find fault with Langston, [a friend said], it is that he wasn't aggressive enough. He was laid-back. You could see passion in his writing, but you never saw it in him. I have never seen him angry.

He was really far too meek for his own good, and far too trusting, [another friend said]. Some people in show business probably thought Langston was sly, that he couldn't possibly be so almost lackadaisical about money and business matters, but that is exactly the way he was. He was not competitive. I would say that he was worldly without being sophisticated, in a sense."

NOT JUST A WRITER

Hughes's mother and brother moved to Washington, D.C., staying with a branch of the Hughes family that settled in the capital. When his mother and D.C. cousins invited him to move in with them, Langston accepted. He didn't have any other plans and he'd be geographically closer to fulfilling his aspirations of attending nearby Howard University. Howard was one of the most prestigious all black schools in the United States during this time, and Hughes's association with Alain Locke would increase his chances of acceptance to the university.

Langston's cousins had read his poems in *The Crisis* and relished having a real poet among them. Hughes didn't return their admiration, and instead barely tolerated them. This branch of the family was well-off, educated, and, Hughes thought, obsessed with fitting into high society. They lived in an elite part of town, associated only with the best people, and often shunned poor, dark-skinned blacks.

Soon after arriving, Hughes discovered that despite his growing reputation, HowardUniversity had no scholarships for him, and Alain Locke was of no help. Rejected, he took a series of jobs, and ended up working as a busboy at the glamorous Wardman Park Hotel.

Throughout these months, Hughes consciously sought out those blacks he considered to be genuine. He walked the poorer black neighborhoods, listening to blues, shooting pool, chatting, and devouring watermelon and barbecue. He listened to black sermons and hymns, always trying to capture the essence of black life, street life—the common music. The legacy of neglect from his parents had left him deeply lonely and eagerly gregarious. He needed these people—the poor, struggling, laughing, and unpretentious black people—to surround him like a family.

He would write anything that came to mind, stick it in a drawer for a few weeks, then look at it again. If he still liked it, he'd send it off to *The Crisis*, *Opportunity*, *Workers Monthly*, *Messenger*, or *Buccaneer*.

That spring, the circle of black writers Hughes was part of was buzzing with excitement about a literary contest sponsored by *Opportunity* magazine, the official organ of the Urban League. He sent in several poems, including his poem "The Weary Blues."

As the announcement date approached, an attack of malaria and a lack of money almost stopped Hughes from attending the awards ceremony in New York. Fauset, sure Hughes had a good shot at winning, lent him the money for the trip. On May 1, 1925, still weak from his illness, he entered the Fifth Avenue restaurant in Manhattan, where a large group of black and white literati were assembled.

The prizes were announced: Hughes's "The Weary Blues" won first prize in poetry. Dozens of Harlem's elite surrounded him, eager to get to know this new black voice. Carl Van Vechten, whom he had met several months earlier, even promised to try to find a publisher for a book of Hughes's poetry. He left Van Vechten a copy of his poems and returned to his busboy job in Washington.

Just two weeks later, he received a telegram from Vechten announcing that Alfred A. Knopf would publish his first book of poetry. Hughes immediately began publicizing the coming book. He gave readings in Washington and New York as often as he could and, with Van Vechten's help, placed several poems in *Vanity Fair*. But Hughes wanted something more spectacular.

He saw his chance when he read that poet Vachel Lindsay would be coming to the Wardman Park Hotel to do a reading. Hughes had admired Lindsay's poetry since high school. He had to meet the man. Quickly writing out three of his poems, Hughes waited for Lindsay to stop by the dining room. He laid the poems next to Lindsay's plate, mumbled his admiration and fled to the kitchen. He watched from behind a pantry door as Lindsay read.

The next morning Hughes was shocked to read in the paper that Lindsay had recited his poems during the reading and talked about the young black poet he'd discovered working as a busboy. When Hughes came to work, a crowd of reporters and photographers, eager to see this new discovery, greeted him. A picture of Hughes dressed in his white serving uniform and carrying a tray stacked with dishes, appeared in most of the city's newspapers. It was the first real publicity Hughes had received outside the black community. Soon, hotel guests were asking Hughes for his autograph.

While waiting for his book to come out, he fell in with a group of eccentric young black men who attended Lincoln University in Pennsylvania. They loved to shock onlookers by walking around barefoot and laughing loudly. They got into white theaters by pretending to be Mexicans. Hughes would prattle loudly in Spanish, while his friends pretended they spoke the language.

It was at this time that Hughes decided to forget about Howard University and instead set his sights on Lincoln— the oldest black university in the country. Lincoln was well respected but had been replaced by Howard as the place for up and coming blacks. It was precisely Lincoln's reputation as a solid but less glamorous institution that attracted Hughes. Many of his literary friends and mentors counseled against the all-black school. He should go to Harvard or Howard, they insisted, where he could make connections in the literary world. Hughes, however, became enthralled by the idea of going to a backwater, all-black school. Just two days after sending his application, Lincoln's dean jumped at the opportunity to have a blossoming poet on campus. All that remained was for Hughes to find the tuition money. Fortunately, just as he was thinking about shipping off to the West Indies, China, or India to make some money, he got a letter from Amy Springarn, a rich white woman he had met earlier, offering him $300 toward his education.

In January 1926 he packed his bags for Lincoln University, a prestigious school nestled in the country 45 miles from Philadelphia. Founded in 1854 by a white abolitionist minister, it had educated more doctors, lawyers, and ministers than any other black college. Students and alumni called it the black Princeton. All the students were black and male. All the professors were white and male, which only increased its distinction among many blacks. But unlike Howard, most of its students were poor, and its alumni were hardly wealthy enough to lavish money on their alma mater.

Just before Hughes arrived at Lincoln, *The Weary Blues* came out. The reviews were good and soon he was inundated with requests for readings and book signings. He read in Washington, New York, and Baltimore, often signing books until his fingers cramped. Wherever he went he tried to make sure his books were being sold in shops patronized by blacks. He also tried to convince Knopf to advertise the book in black publications, although the publisher refused.

The Weary Blues sold well for a first book of poetry by a black man. It sold 1,200 copies quickly and went into a second printing. The New York Times said that the book showed Hughes to be a promising poet.

On campus, Hughes achieved a prominent status. He had a book, awards, and his presence attracted many important visitors. Between studies, social functions, and visitors, he continued to write poems. Soon he had gathered enough for another book. He named this second volume Fine Clothes to the Jew, referring to the black custom of pawning clothing for enough money to make it to the next paycheck.

Early that summer, the editor of The Nation asked Hughes to write a response to an essay the magazine was publishing. The essay ridiculed the idea of a separate black American culture and artistic sense. The editor thought of him for a rebuttal because much of Hughes's work had not only acknowledged, but also reveled in the fact that black culture is unique. His essay, "The Negro Artist and the Racial Mountain," became and remains the quintessential argument for a distinctive black voice, black theme, and black understanding in American art and writing.

Those who denied a separate black sensibility in art, Hughes argued, were giving up pride in their race for pseudo-equality with whites. When a black writer says he just wants to be known as a writer, Hughes said, he's really saying he wants to be white. "The mountain standing in the way of any true Negro art in America [was] this urge within the race toward whiteness," Hughes wrote, "the desire to pour racial individuality into a mold of American standardization, and to be as little Negro and as much American as possible."

With this essay, Hughes publicly declared what he had been doing and would continue to do throughout his career. He was black; he was writing about blacks, for blacks. To capture black culture and black readers was his highest goal. When school let out for the summer, he rented a room in Harlem and fell in with a group of creative, wild young black men known as the Niggerati, joining their whirlwind of parties and shows.

Harlem's streets were bright with nightclubs featuring black singers and dancers. White people flocked to the shows at famous clubs like the Cotton Club and the Savoy, creating a huge market for black entertainers. Black people did all the entertaining but were often barred from the audience. From the outside, Harlem was all glitter and gaiety, but beneath the surface Hughes saw growing resentment.

"So thousands of whites came to Harlem night after night, thinking the Negroes loved to have them there," Hughes said, "and firmly believing that all Harlemites left their houses at sundown to sing and dance in cabarets, because most of the whites saw nothing but cabarets, not the houses."

With the high demand for black theater, Hughes took his first foray onto the stage by writing lyrics for a musical complete with nearly naked chorus girls. The show never made it to production, but it began his lifelong interest in playwriting.

By the following fall Hughes had scraped together the $319 he'd earned on book royalties, a $150 poetry prize from the Poetry Society of America, and a $400 loan from Springarn to pay for another semester at Lincoln.

During Hughes's sophomore year, *Fine Clothes to the Jew* came out. The poems were from the mouths of ordinary black people, and spoke of their everyday lives. They drew on all the long days and nights he had spent on the streets and in the bars and clubs of the poor black neighborhoods. The black intelligentsia exploded. Hughes was called a "sewer dweller," the "poet 'low-rate' of Harlem." His poems were "piffling trash," an "obsession for the more degenerate elements," "a study in the perversions of the Negro."

Hughes had embarrassed them, Rampersad explained, "To these and other black critics, Hughes had allowed the 'secret' shame of their culture, especially its apparently unspeakable or unprintable sexual mores, to be bruited abroad by thick-lipped black whores and roustabouts." Surprised, Hughes shot back, accusing his critics of lacking in artistic and cultural training, suffering low self-esteem, and obsessed with white opinion. Hughes commented:

> The Negro critic and many of the intellectuals were very sensitive about their race in books. (And still are.) In anything that white people were likely to read, they wanted to put their best foot forward, their politely polished and cultural foot—and only that foot. . . .
>
> I sympathized deeply with those critics and those intellectuals, and I saw clearly the need for some of the kinds of books they wanted. But I did not see how they could expect every Negro author to write such books. . . . Anyway, I didn't know the upper class Negroes well enough to write much about them. I knew only the people I had grown up with, and they weren't people whose shoes were always shined, who had been to Harvard, or who had heard of Bach. But they seemed to me good people, too.

The summer after his sophomore year, he met a very rich old widow in New York. Charlotte Mason had an intense passion for Native Americans and blacks and had established a cadre of black artists and writers whom she supported financially. Charlotte was taken with Hughes's polite but profound talent and his Native American and African blood. She offered to be his patron.

More than helping Hughes focus his writing, Charlotte wanted to be part of his journey—merging her vision with his talent. However, Charlotte's vision of the black race was significantly different from his. He wanted black people to achieve equality and enjoy all that America had to offer. Charlotte wanted black people to embrace their primitive side, never acquiescing to modern Western lifestyles and ideas. Hughes would comment:

> Concerning Negroes, she felt that they were America's great link with the primitive, and that they had something very precious to give to the Western World. She felt that there was mystery and mysticism and spontaneous harmony in their souls. . . . She felt that we had a deep well of the spirit within us and that we should keep it pure and deep.

Despite their differences, Hughes accepted Charlotte's offer shortly after starting his junior year at Lincoln. She would send him $150 each month along with gifts for special needs, and he would send her an itemized account of how he spent each check. Hughes's work would be his own, but Charlotte expected to be consulted regularly.

The money transformed Hughes's lifestyle. He bought new suits in Fifth Avenue shops and spent weekends in New York escorting Charlotte to plays, concerts, and lectures. He had only to call her secretary to secure the best seats for any performance. Charlotte often sent gifts to the university— high quality paper, gourmet foods. Hughes soon developed a taste for fine food. Charlotte even financed Gwyn's education for a time, before she realized that Langston's brother was an emotional drain on him.

For Hughes, the emotional bond was the most important part of their relationship. When he was in New York, he spent hours at Charlotte's home, perched on a stool before her queenly chair. Godmother—as she liked to be called—presided, as he and other protégés talked for hours. For him the relationship probably took on overtones of mother–son. He saw in her the support and unconditional love his mother never gave him.

"I was fascinated by her and I loved her," Hughes said. "No one else had ever been so thoughtful of me, or so interested in the things I wanted to do, or so kind and generous toward me."

His own mother, meanwhile, was still the self-indulgent woman who had left her son to grow up lonely and rejected. Now past 50, Carrie still frequented dancehalls and caroused. She often begged Hughes for money and attention. Even her attempts to apologize were tinged with selfishness. "Sometime I feel that you & I were never as close, Heart & heart as we should be," she wrote Hughes, "but I have loved you very dearly and if I failed in some things it was lack of knowledge."

As his junior year ended in 1929, Hughes was overcome by the desire to write a novel. *Not Without Laughter* would be a fictionalized memoir, dealing with his painful childhood memories, but set firmly in an idealized black family. Hughes wrote in a flurry and sent the rough draft to Godmother. She responded with a 24-page letter filled with comments and suggestions. She liked the manuscript but thought that Hughes said too much about social and racial issues. He spent his senior year reworking the novel.

As graduation approached, Hughes was required to conduct a study for a sociology course. He decided to look at students' attitudes about the school's policy of keeping its faculty all white. For some time Hughes had felt Lincoln was becoming mediocre, bending to the wishes of white philanthropists who supported the school. He surveyed the 129 juniors and seniors about their attitudes toward the all-white faculty. A surprising two-thirds wanted to keep black professors out of Lincoln. They said that black professors would be more likely to play favorites and less likely to cooperate with each other. Hughes concluded:

> . . .and the fact that 81 members of the Senior and Junior classes at this college can themselves approve of such a situation, and give reasons for their approval which express open belief in their own inferiority, indicates that the college itself has failed in instilling in these students the very quality of self-reliance and self-respect which any capable American leader should have— and the purpose of this college, let us remember, is to educate leaders of the colored people.

Hughes posted the survey results on a school bulletin board. Someone sent a copy to a black newspaper in Baltimore, which gave the story a front-page headline. A controversy rumbled through Lincoln and spread to other black schools. Several southern black elementary and high school officials wrote to Lincoln announcing they would no longer hire Lincoln graduates. Within 10 years Lincoln would integrate both its faculty and its board of trustees.

In the spring of 1929, Hughes graduated with honors. Still rewriting his novel, he remained at Lincoln to finish it, taking only a short break to work with a small New York theater, writing a play entitled *Mulatto*.

That July, his first novel appeared in bookstores. The reviews were good. *Not Without Laughter* was praised for giving rich texture to the lives of working-class blacks. But Hughes later said that he loathed the book, perhaps because he'd changed it significantly to please Godmother.

With his book finished and Godmother's steady checks, he had a freedom of movement for the first time in a long time. While the country was in the throes of the Great Depression, Hughes was one of the lucky few who could still afford new clothes and theater tickets. When Godmother's chauffeured town car delivered him to the train station, he saw dozens of porters lined up to take baggage. He recognized several of them as fellow students at Lincoln. Although they had studied to be lawyers, writers, and engineers, here they were slinging suitcases. Hughes could feel their eyes on him as he stepped out of the chauffeured car. Part of him liked to show off his good fortune, but another part made him feel like a kept man. He wrote a poem in 1930 entitled "Poet to Patron" that captured some of his feelings:

> What right has anyone to say
> That I Must throw out pieces of my heart for pay?
> For bread that helps to make
> My heart beat true, I must sell myself
> To you?
> A factory shift's better,
> A week's meager pay,
> Than a perfumed note asking
> What poems today?

CARVING OUT INDEPENDENCE

By the winter of 1930, five or six million people were out of work. The homeless, jobless, and hungry became a bedraggled army, sleeping in the subways, standing in bread lines, and begging in the streets. Harlem quickly lost its renaissance. The glamour shows closed up and artists were suddenly out-of work.

One day on the way to Godmother's apartment, Hughes passed by the new Waldorf-Astoria Hotel. After reading announcements of $10 meals and expensive suites, he wrote a poem, "Advertisement of the Waldorf-Astoria," chastising diamond-strewn ladies lounging in luxury while millions suffered. Hughes excitedly showed Godmother the poem. "It isn't you," she snapped after reading it.

With these words Hughes realized that he and Godmother had very different ideas about what he should be writing. Godmother wanted him to write rhythmic stanzas praising his people as noble and wise, while he wanted to change their world. Early in the spring of 1930, he went to her apartment to tell her that he couldn't take her money anymore fully expecting that they would remain friends. He simply didn't want to be beholden, but for Godmother, their relationship was built on money—if Hughes didn't want her money, he wouldn't get her friendship. She launched into a diatribe, accusing him of being ungrateful and of betraying her.

Even years later, Hughes found it difficult to talk about that morning. The most he would say was that "in the end it all came back very near to the old impasse of white and Negro again, white and Negro—as do most relationships in America." Hughes fell ill immediately after this encounter. His tonsils were giving him trouble, his muscles twitched and his stomach turned. He went to the doctor several times, but he knew that his illness, once again, was the result of his anger at being abandoned.

"Violent anger makes me physically ill," he later confessed. "I didn't feel any of those things consciously—for I had loved very much that gentle woman who had been my patron. . . . But now I was violently and physically ill, with my stomach turning over and over each time I thought about that morning at all."

During the next several months, he wrote Godmother again and again begging her to forgive him. In one letter he asks her to "release yourself from the burdens of my own lack of wisdom. . . . The fault is mine, the darkness is mine." He offered to settle their financial accounts and return to a relationship in which money had no part, but Godmother refused to see him.

"That beautiful room, that had been so full of light and help and understanding for me," Hughes said, "suddenly became like a trap closing in, faster and faster, the room darker and darker, until the light went out with a sudden crash in the dark. . . ."

Still feeling ill, Hughes found out that he had won the Harmon Gold Award for Literature and $400 for *Not Without Laughter*. Perhaps, he thought, he could make it on his own. His health improved as did his mindset.

With money in his pocket, Hughes joined his friend, Zell Ingram, on a road trip. Ingram was planning to drive his mother's car to Florida, and Hughes convinced him to continue the trip to Cuba, then Haiti. Hughes had idealized Haiti since childhood and wanted to research the island for a play about its 1791 revolution, that had replaced colonial power and slavery with the first independent black country in the Americas.

When the pair got to Daytona Beach, Florida, they stopped to visit Mary McLeod Bethune. As president of Bethune-Cookman College, Mary was one of the best-known black women in America. She had defied Jim Crow by integrating her classrooms and speaking against segregation.

Bethune asked Hughes to read some of his poems to an English class. She watched as her students hung on his every word. Black students need poetry, Bethune told him. Why not make a speaking tour, taking your poems to schools and universities around the country? Because he desired his poems to be heard by the the average black person, the idea appealed to Hughes. He told her that he would think about it.

From Miami, Ingram and Hughes took a boat to Cuba, then Haiti. They stayed at a small hotel on the waterfront for six months, exploring ruins, listening to fishermen's tales, and mingling with the poor people of Haiti. All the while, Hughes took notes.

Despite Haiti's history of black independence, a rigid social caste separated light and dark-skinned blacks. The light-skinned, wealthy people could afford coats and shoes, which they made a point of wearing at all times. Hughes found it ridiculous to see the upper class sweating under heavy coats and shoes in the hot climate. He was determined to go coatless and shoeless as much as he could. The hotel manager was shocked that a man of Hughes's class would dress so poorly. When he tried to explain, the manager only became more confused.

By July, Hughes and Ingram were almost out of money. They booked passage on a ship back to Florida as deck passengers. When the boat stopped in Port-au-Prince, some of the city's leading writers and officials found out that Hughes was aboard and gathered a delegation, dressed in suits and gloves, to welcome him. They found him on deck, stripped to the waist, barefoot and eating bread, cheese, and wine. Although the delegates didn't say anything, Hughes knew they were shocked by his behavior and dress.

On the return trip, Hughes and Ingram visited Mary McLeod Bethune again. She too was heading to New York and asked to ride with them. Along the way, they stopped at the homes of Bethune's friends to eat and sleep. During one such stop at a black school in South Carolina, the teachers asked Hughes to join them for lunch. When officials heard that he was at the school, however, they stopped classes and called an assembly. Hughes had no choice but to read some poems. The students' response was so enthusiastic, that he could not help but agree with Bethune that black children needed poetry.

When Hughes returned to New York, he immediately got to work organizing a speaking tour. With America in the midst of the Depression he knew that finding work as a writer would be tough. A tour was the perfect solution. He got $1,000 from the Rosenwald Fund to Aid Negro Education and bought a new Model A Ford sedan. Because he didn't know how to drive, he asked a former classmate to come along. Radcliffe Lucas was working as a redcap at Penn Station and jumped at the offer. He would do the driving and get half the profits.

Hughes wrote to every black school and college in the country, offering himself as a speaker. For the larger schools he charged $100 plus room and board. For the smaller schools, he charged $75 or $50. If a school could not afford the fee, he often agreed to come for free.

Hughes and Radcliffe began the tour in October of 1931. Their first stop was at a black boarding school in Pennsylvania, then on to a college in Baltimore, Howard University, then to Virginia. As he moved south, he worked out a stirring presentation. He began by talking about his childhood and reading some of his early poems. Then he moved on to his jazz poems and finally to his most recent ones, dealing with race relations. He ended with "I, too, Sing America."

Most of the students had never met a poet before, let alone a black poet. Hughes stayed and encouraged them after the readings. He set up a book display by other black writers along with copies of *The Weary Blues* and a self-published booklet of his most recent poems, *The Negro Mother*, which he sold for a quarter.

During the tour, Hughes tried to find speaking venues that would reach uneducated blacks. He drove hundreds of miles a week. One day he'd be reading to an audience of cotton pickers, the next to a kindergarten and an old folks home.

It wasn't easy for a black man to travel in the South. Hughes was barred from hotels and often had to stay in private homes along the way. Racism weighed heavily on his mind. He found out that a black staff member at a black college died after a car accident in Georgia because a nearby white hospital refused to treat her. In Alabama a black football coach had been beaten to death by a mob because he mistakenly parked in a white parking lot. Hughes could not understand why the black colleges he spoke at were not incensed by these deaths. He found most of the students and faculty cowardly in their failure to speak out.

One of the worst failures, in his view, was the silence over the Scottsboro case. Nine black boys had been accused of raping two prostitutes on a train in Alabama. Although the evidence was shaky, all except the youngest—a 13-year-old—had been sentenced to death. Hughes wrote several poems and a short play about the case, but he found very few others championing the boys' fate. One of these poems, "Christ in Alabama," would cut through the silence.

He was asked to read at the all-white University of North Carolina in Chapel Hill. Two student editors of the unofficial campus literary paper asked Hughes to send a poem in advance of his visit. He sent "Christ in Alabama," which began, "Christ is a nigger,/Beaten and black." The students printed it the day he arrived. The community exploded. There were rumors that Hughes would be run out of town. The sheriff refused to protect him, saying, "Sure he ought to be run out! It's bad enough to call Christ a *bastard*. But when he calls him a *nigger*, he's gone too far!"

Hughes was not allowed to use the music hall where he was scheduled to speak and instead found a smaller auditorium where the police stood outside in case of trouble. In the wake of the uproar, invitations at white schools stopped, but black audiences filled the halls beyond capacity. Hughes was heralded as the man who had "walked into a lions' den and come out, like Daniel, unscathed."

After speaking at the Tuskegee Institute in Alabama, the chaplain for the Scottsboro boys asked Hughes to read for them. Near Christmas, Hughes entered Kilby Prison and read several of his lighter poems to the boys on death row. Only the youngest smiled. His visit and poems, Hughes said, had been, "futile and stupid in the face of death."

That spring he headed west across Texas, New Mexico, and Arizona to California. The tour had been a success but Hughes was tired. When the Sullivan's, a wealthy white couple, offered to let him stay in their home in Carmel, he thankfully settled in for a few weeks of rest. Their home became a haven for Hughes in the years to come—a place where he was welcome, respected, and able to work.

JOURNEY TO REVOLUTION

While resting at the Sullivan's home, Hughes got a telegram inviting him to join a group of black artists traveling to Russia to produce a movie sponsored by the Union of Soviet Socialist Republics. In 1917, the Russian czarist regime had been overthrown and replaced by a communist system in which the state owned all the property and declared that all people were equal regardless of color, creed, or social class. The U.S.S.R. claimed to be the champion of oppressed people everywhere, and they were eager to prove this to American blacks.

Hughes just made it back to New York before the ship left for Russia. He staggered up the gangplank with his phonograph, typewriter, and a stack of records. When the group got to Moscow, they were treated like stars, staying at the best hotels, eating at the finest restaurants, and going to the best shows—all expenses paid. He hardly noticed the daily inconveniences, the long lines for food, and the mountains of paperwork necessary to accomplish every task.

The script for *Black and White*, written by a Russian playwright who had never been to the United States, was terrible. Black characters were unrealistic caricatures and the story of race relations in the United States was far from accurate. The government canceled the project, but offered to let the group stay and tour the country.

Hughes was eager to see how black people were doing under communism. He got permission to travel as a reporter to Turkmenistan in Central Asia, where most of the brown-skinned Asiatic people lived. The U.S.S.R. had done much to help its backward areas. Before the revolution, nonwhites had been segregated in public places much like blacks in America. Wives were often bought, and Muslim women were required to wear veils. The land was infertile, and the people lived in poverty. Since the revolution, the U.S.S.R. had outlawed segregation and wife buying and instituted dozens of programs designed to educate and reform, but progress was slow.

Eating camel meat and hard bread, Hughes worked his way through the eastern U.S.S.R., writing articles for communist newspapers about the semi-nomadic people he met. He saw shocking poverty, barren state-owned farms, and disease. But he also saw nonwhites being treated with respect and equality. For Hughes, the promise of that equality outweighed the presumably temporary poverty and disease. It was here that he met an Asiatic woman, Sylvia Chen, and began one of the most serious relationships in his life. Long after Hughes had returned to the United States, he and Sylvia continued to correspond.

As he traveled the old caravan routes, a German traveling companion asked Hughes why he did not join the Communist Party. They do not allow jazz, he answered. Because jazz was officially banned as decadent music, Hughes had doubts about communism—he would not give up the music he loved for any revolution.

For Hughes, music was a part of the fabric of life. Everywhere he went he carried his phonograph and a few records. Throughout his career, his poetry would be wedded to black music. He had worked the mood and tempo of jazz into his poetry while in Paris, and would later try to capture the tone of bebop music in words and weave gospel and spirituals into his stage musicals. The music of a people, Hughes believed, told their story, their hopes, their fears and he would always look to music to guide his writing.

In early spring of 1932, Hughes returned to Moscow. He had been in the U.S.S.R. for six months and his visitor's permit expired. With this, he decided to take the long way home—the Trans-Siberian Railway toward Japan.

He rode the train for 10 days across the bleak landscape of the northeastern U.S.S.R., arriving at last in Vladivostok where he boarded a ship for Japan. In Tokyo, Hughes visited other writers and toured the city.

He then headed for a brief trip to Shanghai in China which like the U.S.S.R., had recently become communist. But here Hughes saw that the people were divided along sharply drawn color lines. He was appalled that whites barred the Chinese from many public places in their own country.

From China, Hughes bought a ticket on a ship headed for San Francisco. When the boat stopped at Yokohama, Japan, for three days, he decided to pass the time in nearby Tokyo. On the morning he arrived, he was summoned to the police station and interrogated all day. Why had he been in China and in the U.S.S.R.? What had he seen there? Confounded by the questions, Hughes answered as best he could. He later heard that he was suspected of carrying messages and secret documents from the U.S.S.R. and China to communists in Japan. Police had kept a file detailing all his activities in Shanghai and Tokyo. After a long day, he was told to leave Japan and never to return.

When the ship reached Hawaii, he read news reports about his experiences with the Japanese police. Several false statements had been printed. He was quoted as saying that Japan would be the savior of dark people everywhere and praising their imperialist attitude. Although the false reports angered him, he shrugged them off—unaware that these ideas would be untenable a few years hence.

Hughes returned at the height of the Depression, and he was grateful that Noel Sullivan had once again invited him to stay at his cottage in Carmel. He settled in with Greta, the Sullivan's German shepherd, to write for a year—one of the longest stretches in which he had stayed in one place.

It was a productive year. Hughes wrote dozens of short stories that would be collected in *The Ways of White Folks* in 1934. Many of the stories focused on the ways in which white people controlled black people—whether sharecroppers, janitors, or writers. He plunged into activism with fundraisers, petitions, and picket lines for the Scottsboro boys and California's migrant workers.

He flourished in Carmel and even considered committing to Sylvia Chen, to whom he had been writing during the past year. He had checked into immigration law and asked her to come for a visit. For some reason he never followed through, and she never knew just how close he had came to asking her to marry him.

In the summer of 1934, Hughes's father died. He traveled to Mexico for the reading of the will, from which he was excluded, and decided to spend the winter there. He translated his poems into Spanish, met the country's artists, and frequented bars listening to mariachi guitars. He was broke, hungry, living Bohemian, and loving it.

At the end of the summer, Hughes found out that his mother had breast cancer. He left immediately for Oberlin, Ohio, where Carrie had moved in with distant cousins. Although he had been sending her money regularly, she had given most of it to her cousins. When he won a Guggenheim Fellowship that year, to support his writing, most of it went to pay his mother's medical bills.

To raise more money for his mother's treatment, Hughes headed to New York in the fall to try to sell some stories. When he arrived, he found that a play he had written after his graduation from Lincoln was in rehearsals for a Broadway opening. *Mulatto* told the story of a boy with a black housekeeper mother and a white plantation-owner father. The son kills the father during a fight. A lynch mob comes after the boy, who kills himself before they get him. The mother is driven insane. Watching rehearsals, Hughes was shocked to discover that the producer had made an already bloody play even more sensational. Hughes did not want to risk derailing his first big production, so he kept quiet. He did, however, successfully protest the theater's segregated seating policy.

Mulatto was a hit. It ran for a year in New York—a performance record set by a black playwright that stood for 24 years. Hughes was hooked. When he returned to care for his mother, who was now living in Cleveland, he wrote half a dozen plays in the next year for Cleveland's Karamu Theater. Although he loved the theater, it was frustrating work. There was never enough money and directors, producers, and actors all tried to change his words. So when in the spring of 1937, the *Baltimore Afro-American* newspaper asked him to cover black soldiers involved in the Spanish Civil War, he was delighted to escape the theater.

In the wake of World War I, fascism had arisen in Germany, led by Adolf Hitler, and in Italy, led by Benito Mussolini. When Spain's army officers revolted and set up a military dictatorship under General Francisco Franco, Hitler and Mussolini supported the revolt as an opportunity to forge another alliance. Spain's common soldiers and common people refused to surrender, however, and the civil war became a conflict between the classes. Hughes was eager to support the antifascist resistance fighters.

When he arrived in Barcelona, Spain, after his long trip across the Atlantic, he was so tired that he slept through an air-raid warning and awoke to falling bombs. "The next thing I knew was that, with part of my clothes in my arms, I was running in the dark toward the stairs," Hughes remembered. "A terrific explosion somewhere nearby had literally lifted me out of bed." In the next few weeks, Hughes got accustomed to the bombings. Barcelona and Madrid were the first European cities to be bombed from the air on a massive scale. Spanish cities were helpless because they had no air defenses— thousands of civilians died in the first month.

Hitler and Mussolini sent planes and tanks to Franco's forces while Britain, France, and the United States refused to help the resistance. Despite such refusals on the parts of governments, 40,000 individuals from around the world did come to the aid of the resistance, including hundreds of black Americans who enlisted in the unsegregated International Brigade.

For six months, Hughes lived with the bombs, traveling to the front lines to talk to black volunteers and telling America what he saw. In one report he described entering a small town that had been destroyed by Franco's forces:

> Nobody remained there, but there were still portions of the dead in the streets. Whole bodies had been cleared away, but hands, arms, fingers and legs were still lying around, protruding from piles of rubble, smelling not good in the sun. . . .
>
> Some of the men in the International Brigades had told me they came to Spain to help keep war and fascism from spreading. War and fascism—a great many people at home in America seemed to think those words were just a left-wing slogan. War and fascism! He was not just a slogan, that dead man sprawled on the floor of his house. . . .
>
> Death does not smell good at all, [I thought], a little sick at the stomach as I walked away from that Spanish town where nobody lived any more on account of war and fascism.

In December Hughes decided he should leave. He had written every war story that he could find and was doing nothing but helping to consume what little food the resistance had left—potato peels, sausage skins, and cat meat. By 1939, Franco had crushed the resistance. Of the 3,200 Americans who fought there, 1,800 were killed and most of the rest were wounded.

A Poet's Politics

In January 1938, Hughes returned to New York broke and anxious to return to the theater. But rather than write plays and hope that one would find its way to the mostly white audiences on Broadway, he decided to start his own Harlem theater group. With money from the International Workers Order, Hughes created a uniquely black theater. He hired black actors, writers, directors, and set designers and converted a second-story loft into the Harlem Suitcase Theater—so named because all their equipment could be squeezed into a suitcase.

The first play was Hughes's *Don't You Want to Be Free?* —an epic, poetic look at black culture from slavery to modern life, interwoven with spirituals and jazz. He wanted not just to entertain the audience but to educate them as well. He adopted a staging technique he had seen in the U.S.S.R. called theater-in-the-round. With no curtains, actors and singers performed on a round platform encircled by the audience. Tickets were only 35 cents and shows were performed on weekends only, when working people could come. There were 135 performances—the longest consecutive run ever recorded in Harlem.

While Hughes was in Spain, his mother's cancer had spread to her lungs. She moved to New York to be near him during her final days, and on June 3, at the age of 65, Carrie died. He had to borrow from a friend to pay for her funeral.

By 1939, the Suitcase Theater was well established and Hughes headed to Los Angeles to start another black theater group. He called this group the New Negro Theater and again opened with *Don't You Want to Be Free?*

While Hughes was working on the play, his friend, Clarence Muse, asked him to help with a Hollywood screenplay. Hollywood was notoriously off limits to black writers, but Clarence had managed to impress the right people and landed a job developing a film for a popular singer. The movie would be set in the South as a black-boy, white-boy version of Tom Sawyer and Huck Finn; it was entitled *Way Down South*.

Hughes was thrilled. He would earn $1,200 for three months work and would be able to pay the debt he still owed for his mother's funeral. But Hollywood was a demeaning place to work. He had to drive for miles to get to work every day because blacks were not welcome at apartments close to the studios. He once had to eat a sandwich outside in the sweltering heat because several white movie executives refused to enter a restaurant with him.

"Hollywood is our bête noire," Hughes said. "It is America (and the world's) most popular art. . . . Yet, shamelessly and to all the world since its inception, Hollywood has spread in exaggerated form every ugly and ridiculous stereotype of the deep South's conception of Negro character."

In early April he finished *Way Down South*. After a brief speaking tour, he settled in with the Sullivan's again to finish an autobiography he had worked on sporadically for several years. The Sullivan's had built Hughes a one-room cottage on their farm. It was the closest Hughes had ever come to having a home. The autobiography, *The Big Sea*, came out to fantastic reviews. The book was honest—not bitter—real, and sensitive. But sales were slow. It was also during this time that he revised a collection of poems, *Shakespeare in Harlem*. Despite having several books in print (his latest one a critical success) and despite the generosity of the Sullivan's, Hughes was still not financially secure, and he had to borrow $50 when his teeth needed work.

While Hughes continued his writing, America was entering its "red scare" period, and Langston Hughes's ties to the U.S.S.R. were about to hurt him. The attacks he suffered in the coming years would often center on a poem he wrote while traveling in the Soviet Union in 1932. A friend had published it without his permission. "Goodbye Christ" was meant to point a finger at evangelists who seemed more interested in making money than leading people to Christ. In part, the poem read:

> Listen Christ,
> You did alright in your day, I reckon—
> But that day's gone now.
> They ghosted you up a swell story, too,
> Called it the Bible—
> But it's dead now.
> The popes and the preachers've
> Made too much money from it.
> They've sold you to too many. . . .
>
> Goodbye,
> Christ Jesus Lord God Jehovah,
> Beat it on away from here now.
> Make way for a new guy with no religion at all—
> A real guy named
> Marx Communist Lenin peasant Stalin worker ME. . . .

These troubles began in November 1940. When Hughes appeared for a luncheon speech at the swank Vista del Arroyo Hotel in Pasadena, California, protesters mobbed him. A sound truck blared "God Bless America" and a hundred people, led by the notorious evangelist, Aimee Semple McPherson, were picketing him. The organizers had printed "Goodbye Christ" on leaflets, denouncing him as a communist. Perhaps even more shocking was the fact that several black preachers had joined the protest. Police tried to disperse the protesters, but the crowd refused to leave. The chief of police eventually escorted Hughes through the mob and back to Los Angeles.

While heading back to Carmel in December to escape the barrage, Hughes picked up a copy of the *Saturday Evening Post*. Inside it was a reprint of the Pasadena leaflet, accusing him of being a communist, as well as a reprint of "Goodbye Christ." He immediately wrote a statement repudiating the poem. I "would not and could not write such a poem now," he wrote. He sent the statement to all his accusers. He tried to stop people from reprinting the poem, but his lawyers told him that the poem was now in the public domain.

Similar outrage was building throughout the country. In Detroit, Mothers of America picketed him. In Gary, Indiana, a group of black teachers were threatened with losing their jobs if they didn't renege on their invitation for Hughes to speak at a public school. Everywhere he went, Langston Hughes was likely to be met with a protest. "It's been a running feud with Klan-minded censors from Florida to California who like neither poetry nor Negroes," Hughes said after completing 45 speaking engagements, often marred by protests.

Hughes was fighting for his career. He knew that to be identified with the left would quash his ability to get work published in mainstream presses. He also knew he had to protect his reputation to protect his work, yet his attempts to save his reputation angered the left who saw him as a traitor. The *Communist People's World*, a magazine that had long supported Hughes, turned against him for denouncing the poem. "So goodbye Hughes," they wrote. "This is where you get off."

At the end of 1940, Hughes felt like a financial and artistic failure. *The Big Sea* had only sold 2,845 copies, his speaking engagements had dried up, and he was sick—eventually spending several weeks in the hospital suffering from gonorrhea. He was released from the hospital on his 39th birthday, still weak and groggy. With his illness and the rebuff he had received over "Goodbye Christ," Hughes sank into depression. He questioned whether it was possible for a black man to earn a living with his pen. As Rampersad wrote:

> Perhaps the most glowing feature of his personality, both as an individual and an artist, had been his power to invoke and exude a luminously childlike sense of innocence and wonder. But the passage of years and events had contaminated this gift of innocence. In any event, in spite of his grandmother's noble lessons about resistance, he had been a lonely child. Now, for all of his striking accomplishments and thousand friends, he was a lonely man.

He canceled all his speaking engagements, propped himself up in bed, and began the second volume of his autobiography. The work was cathartic, and by the following year he was again ready to plunge into theatrical work. He moved to Chicago in 1941 to found another theater group, the Skyloft

Players. They opened with a historical play he had written about the Underground Railroad, *The Sun Do Move*.

Although the Harlem and Los Angeles theaters did not last, the Chicago one did. Hughes's work in forming black theater groups would be continued by others in the years to come. These theaters gave writers an outlet for their work and gave starts to some of America's best black actors.

Hughes was reviewing proofs of his latest book of poetry, *Shakespeare in Harlem*, in December 1941, when he heard that the Japanese had bombed Pearl Harbor. Twenty-one vessels were sunk or badly damaged, almost 200 airplanes were destroyed, and approximately 3,000 naval and military personnel were killed or wounded. America, previously reluctant to join in the European fighting, was about to go to war.

Hughes believed that America's entry into the war presented an opportunity to gain equality for blacks at home. When President Roosevelt had signed a declaration forbidding discrimination in government and defense industry jobs, Hughes's optimism blossomed. He wrote the poem, "Jim Crow's Last Stand," which partially read, "Pearl Harbor put Jim Crow on the run." At least that was what he hoped.

That summer Hughes returned to Harlem and threw himself into the war effort. He wrote slogans for the Treasury Department's effort to sell war bonds, and articles telling the country what blacks were doing in the services. He joined other well-known writers on an advisory board of the Writers' War Committee, which volunteered to help with the war effort. He even wrote patriotic war songs. While he received no payment for his work, Langston Hughes was proving to his detractors that he was no communist— he loved his country.

In late October, Hughes received a draft questionnaire in the mail. Although he was 40, the country had become desperate for soldiers and was calling on men usually considered past fighting age. He dutifully filled out the questionnaire, marking himself as white, Negro, and Indian, and attached a statement protesting questions about race:

> I wish to register herewith, as a citizen of the United States, my complete disapproval of the segregating of the armed forces of the United States into White and Negro units, thus making the colored citizens the only American group so singled out for Jim Crow treatment, which seems to me contrary to the letter and spirit of the Constitution and damaging to the morale and well-being of not only the colored citizens of this country but millions of our darker allies as well.

Hughes was listed 1-A, a prime candidate for drafting. He managed to get a 60-day deferment to go on a planned lecture tour, which included appearances at several Armed Services organizations. In February, as Hughes turned 41, President Roosevelt signed an order deferring the draft for all men over age 38. Hughes was off the hook. With his freedom intact, he renewed his efforts to use the war to point the way toward equality for black people. He settled in Harlem, feeling a need to root himself in a community of black people. Several weeks earlier, the *Chicago Defender* newspaper had offered him $15 a week to write a column. He called it "From Here to Yonder," and explained that it would be about far away events affecting people at home.

Much of his work in the early 1940s was patriotic and optimistic. In a 1943 essay, "My America," Hughes wrote about the injustices blacks suffered in America. He continued, "Yet America is a land where, in spite of its defects, I can write this article. Here the voice of democracy is still heard. . . . And we know it is within our power to help in its further change toward a finer and better democracy than any citizen has known before. The American Negro believes in democracy."

While Hughes remained optimistic, he saw that other black writers were slipping into pessimism, focusing on the pain and suffering of racism, not the triumphs, the heroes, or the possibility of change. Hughes warned about this dangerous trend:

> If the best of our writers continue to pour their talent into the tragedies of frustration and weakness, tomorrow will probably say, on the basis of available literary evidence, No wonder the Negroes never amounted to anything. There were no heroes among them. Defeat and panic, moaning, groaning, and weeping were their lot. Did nobody fight? Did nobody triumph?

On a night in January 1943 Hughes was drinking beers at Patsy's Bar and Grill in Harlem with a man and his girlfriend. He asked the man what he did for a living. The man answered that he made cranks.

"What kind of cranks?" Hughes asked.

"Cranks," the fellow replied. "Cranks. Just cranks!"

His girlfriend chimed in, "You been working in that war plant long enough," she drawled. "You ought to know what they crank."

"I do not know!"

Hughes and the girlfriend wondered out loud how he could make cranks and not know what they were for.

The man answered, how could they not know that white folks never tell blacks what they are making. "I don't crank with those cranks," he said. "I just make 'em."

"You sound," his girlfriend snapped, "right simple."

With those words, Simple was born. "Out of the mystery as to what the cranks of the world crank, to whom they belong and why," Hughes said, he created the character of Simple, "wondering and laughing at the numerous problems of white folks, colored folks, and just folks—including himself."

A few days later, Simple appeared in Hughes's weekly *Defender* column. For three weeks, readers saw a running conversation between Simple, an uneducated, curiously wise, racially defensive and amusing black man, and an educated, stuffy, proper liberal black narrator. For the next 23 years, he would write about Simple, producing five books and numerous columns, dealing with everything from love to lynching, and intermarriage to international affairs.

Simple became so popular and captured the tension between races with such honesty and humor that one black critic commented, "If you want to understand the black brother, learn to know Simple."

Simple, Hughes wrote, is "really very simple. It is just myself talking to me. Or else me talking to myself . . . I felt that by writing honestly enough and truthfully enough and beautifully enough about *one* man in *one* place on *one* corner, 125th and Lenox, people around the world might recognize him as being one of them, no mater where they lived."

"WORRIATION OVER A POET"

In April 1943 Hughes set out on another speaking tour. He had been writing about the treatment of Japanese Americans who were shipped to internment camps as the war with Japan intensified. He wrote in support of Mohandas Gandhi's campaign to rid India of British rule. He wrote a farcical essay about segregation, "White Folks Do the Funniest Things." None of these works endeared Hughes to the right-wing forces that were against him because of "Goodbye Christ."

At Wayne University in Detroit, phone calls to university officials threatened trouble if Hughes spoke there. Hughes arrived to find a picket line of almost 100 people from the America First Party handing out leaflets condemning him as "an atheistic communist, a self-confessed communist and a notorious blasphemous poet."

With a police escort Hughes made it through the line and into a packed auditorium. He countered the picketers, saying, "I am for Christianity that fights poll tax, race discrimination, lynching, injustice and inequality of the masses. I don't feel that religion should be used to beat down Jews [and] Negroes, and to persecute other minority groups." The audience gave him a standing ovation.

Despite run-ins with protesters, the tour went so well that Hughes contemplated a longer tour aimed at white audiences. No black speaker had ever broken into the top level of the lecture circuit.

Meanwhile he was asked to participate in an NBC radio debate, "Let's Face the Race Question," about whether the government should interfere to stop segregation. Hughes did not consider himself a quick thinker and was nervous about the debate. He prepared well and came across as natural. He used humor to put his opponents on the defensive and to secure his standing as a humble but aggressive fighter against segregation. This performance opened the doors to the white lecture circuit. The most prestigious speakers bureau in the country accepted him as the first black person on their roster.

In the next few months, Hughes made at least 50 appearances from Chicago to Virginia, and Kansas to Arizona. He was allowed to stay at previously white-only hotels. When protesters in Flint threatened to disrupt his lecture, audience support was so strong that they moved to an auditorium twice as large.

However, there were sobering moments too. When he and several white friends tried to eat at a Chinese restaurant in Flint, the owner refused to seat Hughes. In his usual civil but direct manner, Hughes questioned the Chinese man, who explained that he was worried that other customers would leave if he let a black man in.

Hughes later wrote the owner a letter. "As I told you that night, I have been in China and I have seen their white English and American people who have set up the same kind of discrimination against you. I very much regret that you in this country contribute to the further humiliation of your colored brothers."

Even when confronting discrimination, Hughes was even-tempered and forgiving. He was nice when confronting Jim Crow, walking barefoot on the beach with friends, working with gruff sailors, selling an idea to a publisher, or talking to students after a lecture. As Rampersad wrote:

> In all my years of research on his life, it was very, very hard to find anyone who had known him who would say a harsh thing about him. . . . The truth is that people who knew him could remember little that wasn't pleasant. Evidently, he radiated joy and humanity, and this was how he was remembered after his death.

The tour paid off financially. In April 1944, for the first time in his 23 years of writing, Hughes's bank account held more than $1,000. He felt that he was on the brink of something close to prosperity and a settled life. This feeling would not last. On August 14 Japan surrendered and the war was over. Hughes had pinned his hopes on the belief that the changes wrought by war would catalyze changes in America's attitudes toward black people. They did not. In his *Defender* column, Hughes wrote:

> I would have my country know that what we have here of Hitler should have gone long ago. I would have my country know that there is no truth in the false differences of blood, and no democracy in the false limitations of opportunities because of race, and no justice in segregated buses and trains, and no decency in a separate Army and Navy. I regret my country did not learn more quickly, but I never really expected bullets and bombs three thousand miles away to be good teachers. The dead never know what hit them, and the wounded seldom realize that their own collective failings at home helped make the bullets that struck them down.

In the midst of his disappointment, Knopf, which had published several of Hughes's books, rejected his latest collection of poems. A Knopf official later recalled how the publishing house often snubbed him:

> When Wallace Stevens visited the office, people were in awe of him. We treated him like a lord. Hardly anybody cared about Hughes. As far as I am concerned, he wrote baby poetry, poor stuff. If we had to go out to lunch with him, say to a French restaurant in mid-town, it was kind of embarrassing. He was a nice enough guy, but you couldn't get around the race thing.

As Hughes toured, taught, and wrote, his optimism diminished and his disillusionment with the pace of progress toward equality deepened.
In 1951 he finished a new book of poems steeped in his disappointment, *Montage of a Dream Deferred*. He asked, "What happens to a dream deferred?/Does it dry up/ like a raisin in the sun?" America was not ready for such questions.

In the fallout of World War II, the Soviet Union had become the new common enemy. Anyone who criticized America or spoke well of communism was suspect. A group of politicians and government officials were determined to root out American communism before it infected the country. The House of Representatives Special Committee on Un-American Activities was their primary tool.

The FBI began investigating Hughes in 1940 during the uproar over "Goodbye Christ." Since that time, the FBI had amassed numerous erroneous "facts" about him. They said that he was a member of the Communist Party, that he had run for public office, called for a race war, married a white woman, and studied communism in the U.S.S.R. They had checked his draft records, riffled through his mail, scrutinized his friends, and questioned the superintendent of his apartment building.

In 1944 the Committee on Un-American Activities declared Hughes "an avowed Communist" and read "Goodbye Christ" into the record as part of the evidence against him. Attacks came from everywhere. Newspapers and magazines blasted Hughes as a traitor. Speaking requests were canceled. Protests at his lectures increased. At some stops he did not even attempt to speak because of the protesting mobs. Hughes gave rebuttals during speaking engagements and placed them in newspapers and magazines, but the fervor against him grew.

"If I were a loud speaking gentleman. . . delivering some world-shaking message or a politician running for office, it would throw a different light on the matter," he said. "But all this worriation over a poet."

And so it continued into the 1950s, when Senator Joseph McCarthy took up the anticommunism cause and became its most strident, paranoid force. Hughes walked a tightrope, trying to keep himself out of the firing line while using his words to change his country. It was of little use as anyone fighting for change in America became a target.

Hughes was in his third-floor office finishing up a children's book when a United States marshal served him with a subpoena in May 1953. He was ordered to appear before the Committee on Un-American Activities. He had two choices. He could cooperate or he could refuse to testify. Many other artists had refused and been jailed for contempt of court. For Hughes, the choice was clear, if not easy. He could not let his work languish while he sat in jail. He would try to negotiate a middle ground—cooperating just enough to avoid jail but not so much as to betray his ideals. He wrote a five-page statement over the weekend. Hughes flew to Washington, and at 10:30 A.M. on Thursday, March 26, appeared amid the glare of television lights and radio microphones before McCarthy's committee. His statement was accepted into the record:

> Some of my earliest poems were social poems in that they were
> about people's problems—whole groups of people's problems—
> rather than my own personal difficulties, but when one writes

poems of social content there is always the danger of being misunderstood. . . .

Perhaps the most misunderstood of my poems was "Goodbye Christ." Since it is an ironic poem (and irony is apparently a quality not readily understood in poetry by unliterary minds) it has been widely misinterpreted as an anti-religious poem. This I did not mean it to be, but rather a poem against racketeering, profiteering, racial segregation, and showmanship in religion which, at the time, I felt was undermining the foundations of the great and decent ideals for which Christ himself stood. . . .

I do not believe in a static America. I believe in an America that changes as Americans want it to change. I do not believe that the desire for change, and working toward it, is necessarily un-American. . . .

I would like to see an America where people of any race, color or creed may live on a plane of cultural and material well-being . . . an America proud of its tradition, capable of facing the future without the necessary pitting of people against people and without the disease of personal distrust and suspicion of one's neighbor. . .

Hughes's statement and subsequent questioning was a tour de force. He had blasted the anticommunist attackers, calling them uneducated, paranoid, and vindictive. Not once had he denounced the communist ideals that he still admired. He had spoken honestly and with dignity, disarming McCarthy and protecting the special literary place he had so painstakingly carved out.

After more than 10 years of defending his ideas and work, Hughes was tired of it. "I have been accused of such membership so often," he wrote after the American Legion in New York accused him of belonging to communist organizations the next year, "that I have gotten used to it, know that the accusers pay no attention to denials, and therefore I pay no attention to their accusations."

Hughes continued to do what he had been doing for decades, piecing together a living from speechmaking and numerous forms of writing. He was frustrated by having to dabble in so many things to make a living.

I get back to Harlem from California, [Hughes said], to find two years of unfinished commitments clouding the Eastern skies with gloom—ranging from books to operas for which nobody has given enough to cover working time adequately—and dreaming time and creative time NOT AT ALL. (Colored are supposed to do in two months what white folks take 2 years for, or more.)

Even with so little creative time, Hughes was prolific during the 1950s. He wrote a book of short stories, *Laughing to Keep from Crying*, two more Simple books, and the second volume of his autobiography, *I Wonder As I Wander*. He wrote a gospel musical for Broadway, *Black Nativity*; a folk musical, *Tambourines to Glory*; and a novel by the same name. In 1958 a compilation of his work, *Langston Hughes Reader*, was published. He published children's books about famous black Americans in 1952 and 1954. In 1959, Knopf published *Selected Poems of Langston Hughes* and in 1961, *Ask Your Mama*.

As the decade progressed, a new crop of black writers began achieving the kind of success that Hughes never had. The change had begun in 1940 with Richard Wright's *Native Son*. In 1952, Ralph Ellison exploded onto the literary scene with *Invisible Man*. The next year James Baldwin's *Go Tell It on the Mountain* appeared. In 1959 Lorraine Hansberry's play, *A Raisin in the Sun*, was produced (its title borrowed from one of Hughes's poems). Meanwhile, poet Gwendolyn Brooks won the Pulitzer Prize. Many of these works were earning their authors large advances and royalties while Hughes still struggled. At Christmas of 1958, Hughes had $9.04 in his bank account.

He did not like the tone of many of the new black writers. They were harsh, barbed, and Hughes felt that they did little to bring about real change in America. But he was careful to keep his criticism to himself. When Baldwin did not do the same for him and criticized *Selected Poems* in "The New York Times Review," Hughes felt betrayed. Baldwin's review noted:

> Every time I read Langston Hughes, I am amazed all over again by his genuine gifts—and depressed that he had done so little with them. . . . [His] poems which take refuge, finally, in a fake simplicity in order to avoid the very difficult simplicity of experience. . . he has not forced them into the realm of art where their meaning would become clear and overwhelming. . . . Hughes is an American Negro poet and has no choice but to be acutely aware of it. He is not the first American Negro to find the war between his social and artistic responsibilities all but irreconcilable.

Baldwin's words stung. Hughes had always rooted his poems in black experience. He had written about blacks for blacks and his inspiration came from the black struggle. Now Hughes felt he was being eclipsed by a new batch of writers who saw his work as outmoded.

He lightheartedly retaliated. Every time he got a request for a free appearance at a school or organization, Hughes declined, but suggested that the wonderful author, Mr. James Baldwin, might be interested. He made sure to give Baldwin's home address and phone number. Years later, Baldwin admitted that he had not really read the book and that Hughes's writing had been crucial in helping him understand himself and black culture.

While Hughes was feeling like a has-been, he turned his attention away from blacks in America and toward blacks in Africa. Throughout his life he had reached out to people of color in other countries—the Caribbean, Mexico, South America, Spain—translating their work into English and bringing it to American readers. Now he would do the same for African writers. He contacted every young writer he could find in Africa, asking them to submit work for an anthology of the best young African writers. He carefully collected and edited their manuscripts for two years.

In 1960 colonial Africa was breaking up. Countries were shrugging off European control and creating independent, black-run countries. The upheaval brought Africa to the center of world attention and made publishers eager to get in on the movement. Hughes found a publisher for *An African Treasury: Articles, Essays, Stories, Poems by Black Africans*, which was promptly banned in South Africa.

During the early 1960s, he would return to Africa several times, attending the inauguration of a new black leader in Nigeria, participating in a festival of African culture sponsored by American blacks, and representing the United States in Ghana at the dedication of a U.S. Information Service Center and Library.

In 1966, President Lyndon B. Johnson appointed Langston Hughes the American representative to the First World Festival of Negro Arts in Dakar, Senegal. The festival featured such American black artists as the Alvin Ailey dance troupe, Duke Ellington, and gospel singer Marion Williams. But Hughes was the most celebrated American. The *New York Times* reported "young writers from all over Africa followed him about the city and haunted his hotel the way American youngsters dog favorite baseball players."

Hughes considered the appointment one of the greatest honors of his life. The festival was exhilarating. But afterward when he traveled Africa on his own, he became disappointed with the newly independent African nations. He saw corruption and the threat of coups everywhere, but he believed that in time democracy would take root.

Meanwhile, at home, the civil rights movement progressed. The loose, scattered fight for equality had organized into groups—a far more effective approach.

On May 17, 1954, the Supreme Court, in *Brown v. Board of Education* of Topeka, Kansas, ruled that segregation in the country's schools was against the law. In December 1955, Rosa Parks refused to give up her bus seat to a white man as the law in Montgomery, Alabama, demanded, starting a boycott that kicked off a nationwide civil rights struggle. A young black minister from Atlanta, Reverend Martin Luther King Jr. became the movement's leader.

America reacted violently to the changes. Marches and rallies were met with clubs and tear gas. Blacks were lynched and black churches bombed. With civil rights at the forefront of the nation's problems, Hughes found himself in vogue again. Publications and organizations sought him out as a well-mannered, well-known black who understood the issues. He doubled his speaking fees and jumped into the fray.

Hughes was a good spokesman for the cause. He believed that black writing, now more than ever, had a crucial place in guiding blacks and whites through the turmoil. "Colored literature in these days of integration will help whites understand the transition," he said, "help them learn that colored Americans are like any other people; help our children to know our contribution to the struggle and development of America, and help white children gain respect for colored people."

On June 26, 1960, he won the N.A.A.C.P.'s annual Springarn Medal. For years Hughes had been overlooked, now he was exalted. In accepting the award, he spoke about what it meant to be a *black* writer. "Yet there are some of us who say, 'Why write about Negroes? Why not be *just a writer*?' And why not—if one wants to be 'just a writer?' Negroes in a free world should be whatever each wants to be—even it means being 'just a writer'. . . .

"So I would say to young Negro writers, do not be afraid of yourself. You are the world. . . ."

As the civil rights movement, centering on nonviolent civil disobedience, continued, some blacks became frustrated with the slow gains and backlash. In the 1960s a new faction arose which became known as the black power movement. It rejected such polite means and called for using violence to change America. Led by Malcolm X, the movement also believed that whites had no legitimate place in the struggle.

Hughes, who had relied on and befriended whites all his life, detested this new thinking. His entire work had been based on his belief that people were people and that making a distinction based on color was absurd. The black power movement spawned a new breed of artist, who was shrill and angry. Hughes responded by calling the movement's art "fingerpainting in excrement."

Meanwhile, Harlem continued its downward slide. Crime and drugs had left their mark and people were afraid to venture into some of its neighborhoods.

> At the end of his life, he was proud to be (according to his reckoning) the only major African American writer still living in the midst of a typical urban black community, and not in a suburb or in voluntary, comfortable exile in Turkey or Spain or some similar place, [Rampersad said]. He was very proud that his life and career had been linked indissolubly with the African American world.

Hughes understood the change and remained loyal to Harlem. But the threat of violence seemed to him to seethe just beneath the surface of everything. As he explained to a friend:

> You see, I love Harlem. I've lived all over the world and I still find it's one of the most beautiful places I know. But the younger people don't feel this way. History is finally catching up with America. Still, I hate to see the anger in the young faces all the time—it's even hard for me to write my Simple stories anymore. There's so much bitterness and anger that they don't seem to be as funny as they used to.

In 1966, after 25 years, Hughes decided Simple had to go. "The racial climate has gotten so complicated and bitter that cheerful and ironic humor is less and less understandable to many people," he said. "A plain, gentle kind of humor can so easily turn people cantankerous, and you get so many ugly letters."

In Simple's last appearance, he bought a house in a white suburb and listened to his wife nag him about how hard he would have to work to keep the yard looking good, so white folks would see that a black family could keep up appearances just as well.

Hughes wondered if anybody was even listening to a mild, aging poet anymore. It seemed that his gentle persuasion was being drowned out by invective. He read in the *Harlem Liberator*, the voice of the black protest movement, that he was unable to "communicate his 'negroness'. It is as if he is saying to 'make it' in this white man's world one has to sacrifice one's blackness."

Despite such obstacles, Hughes felt he had no other choice but to continue throwing his words into the vortex of the events of his time. "A poet is a human being," he wrote in a personal manifesto he never published.

"Each human being must live within his time, with and for his people, and within the boundaries of his country. Therefore, how can a poet keep out of politics?

Hang yourself, poet, in your own words. Otherwise, you are dead."

In 1965, he wrote a column for the *New York Post*, "Taxi, Anyone," about how drivers systematically refused to pick up black customers and bypassed Harlem altogether. The column drew more nasty mail than any other. "I think you belong with that other moron Malcolm X," said one. "Get a hack license and pick up your animal friends in your beautiful hometown, Harlem," went another.

The following year he wrote his most militant book of poetry, *The Panther and the Lash*. Its title poem, "Black Panther," spoke about blacks taking violent revenge against white oppression. The book was Hughes's way of telling the younger generation that he was still there, still fighting.

On May 6, 1967, Hughes was at a dinner party when a severe pain stabbed his lower abdomen. For several hours he endured, then called a doctor who advised him to go to the emergency room immediately. Tests found tumors in his bladder and his prostate gland. Although they were not cancerous, he was scheduled for surgery to remove the prostate nodules. After the surgery an infection set in. By May 22 his heart was failing; fluid filled his lungs and he became comatose. His pulse rate rocketed, his blood pressure fell, and he stopped breathing at 10:40 P.M., with only a nurse by his side.

The next morning, the front page of the *New York Times* announced Langston Hughes's death to a shocked world. He was only 65 and nobody knew he was sick. Harlem gathered for the memorial service, which he had scripted. A jazz trio played "Do Nothing Till You Hear From Me," and then the packed room listened to Hughes's final words to them:

> Tell all my mourners
> To Mourn in red—
> Cause there ain't no sense
> In my bein' dead.

MATT LONGABUCCO

The Poetics and Prose of Langston Hughes

When the time came for his Lincoln, Illinois, grammar school class to elect a Class Poet, Langston Hughes was the unanimous choice. He had never written a poem before. But he was one of the two African-American students in the class, and, as Hughes recalls in his autobiographical volume *The Big Sea*, "In America most white people think, of course, that all Negroes can sing and dance, and have a sense of rhythm. So my classmates, knowing that a poem had to have rhythm, elected me . . ."

Little did Hughes's classmates, or Hughes himself, realize that he would one day transform their quaintly racist criteria into an aesthetic program drawn from African-American tradition, representing African-American life, and consciously geared toward an African-American audience. In the process, Hughes would often spark controversy and elicit strong reactions from blacks and whites, radicals and conservatives, fellow authors and literary critics, activists and bigots.

Over the course of his 46-year literary career, Hughes proved himself to be a versatile man of letters. Although his popular reputation rests on his poetry, anyone who undertakes a serious reading of Hughes's work will soon find herself negotiating short stories, novels, essays, humorous pieces, journalism, autobiography, drama, song lyrics, translations, criticism, biography, and poetry for children. Many critics have pointed to the unevenness of this large body of work, and parts of it have remained largely ignored in critical estimation. Hughes, for his part, remained prolific throughout his life, perhaps following the blues ethos of necessary perseverance in adversity that he so often evinced in his work.

Hughes's public career began in 1921, the year his poem "The Negro Speaks of Rivers" was published in W.E.B. Du Bois's journal *The Crisis*. It was an auspicious beginning, since the poem would become among his best known, as well as his most-anthologized piece. The timing, too, was perfect; the 19-year-old Hughes arrived in Harlem just as the 1920s were getting underway, and he would be there to witness, as well as help to shape, the so-called "Harlem Renaissance" of African-American music and arts. This fertile period was partly a result of the Great Migration of African Americans from the Jim Crow South to the industrial North, creating a dense pool of talent that included artists like jazz trumpeter Louis Armstrong, novelists Zora Neale Hurston and Nella Larsen, entertainer Josephine Baker, and poet Countee Cullen. The popular explosion of black culture, centered around jazz and Harlem itself, lasted until the stock market crash of 1929 and the Great Depression that followed.

Part of what made the experience new was the influx of white enthusiasts and curiosity seekers who flooded Harlem's nightclubs, bought jazz and blues records, and paid attention to black literature. Suddenly, African-American artists were presented with the unexpected problem of a white audience. Within the Harlem community, some artists were being criticized for portraying African Americans in the stereotypical modes that white audiences had come to expect. Even among those who agreed to present black culture as it really was, there was a vocal faction which advocated the portrayal of only those members of the community—the well-educated, law-abiding, middle and upper classes—who showed African Americans to their best advantage, and thus represented a challenge to established prejudices. In 1926, Hughes addressed these concerns publicly in an essay entitled "The Negro Artist and the Racial Mountain." There he established an artistic credo that he would uphold for the rest of his life.

In his essay, Hughes implicitly argues that the integration of African Americans into America at large must not come at the expense of their own culture and tradition. And it is only by the preservation of black culture that an African American can produce an authentic art:

> One of the most promising of the young Negro poets said to me once, "I want to be a poet—not a Negro poet," meaning, I believe, "I want to write like a white poet"; meaning subconsciously, "I would like to be a white poet"; meaning behind that, "I would like to be white." And I was sorry the young man said that, for no great poet has ever been afraid of

being himself. And I doubted then that, with his desire to run away spiritually from his race, the boy would ever be a great poet. But this is the mountain standing in the way of any true Negro art in America—this urge within the race toward whiteness, the desire to pour racial individuality into the mold of American standardization, and to be as little Negro and as much American as possible.

The argument Hughes is reacting to seems reasonable enough—if we want to live in equality, let us write as though we were equal. Yet Hughes has no illusions about equality; how can he, seeing his fellow Harlemites working as busboys and elevator operators, making a lower wage and paying higher rents than their white counterparts, and being driven to drink and prostitution. Furthermore, Hughes—who counted Walt Whitman and the Whitmanesque Carl Sandburg among his conscious influences—knows that only by responding honestly to the life he finds around him can he make great art. Unlike the self-hating, middle-class blacks that he sees as wanting to be like whites, Hughes announces his intention to find beauty in the traditions and both the good and bad experiences of his people.

Hughes says he is prepared to let white audiences take or leave his work. But again and again he returns to his frustrations with his black audience: "... after every reading I answer questions like these from my own people: Do you think Negroes should always write about Negroes? I wish you wouldn't read some of your poems to white folks. How do you find anything interesting in a place like a cabaret? Why do you write about black people? You aren't black. What makes you do so many jazz poems?" Despite this tide of disapproval, Hughes cannot ignore the thematic richness of race relations: "... when [the black artist] chooses to touch on the relations between Negroes and whites in this country with their innumerable overtones and undertones, surely ... there is an inexhaustible supply of themes at hand." He cites Jean Toomer (the author of *Cane*), Du Bois, and the singer Paul Robeson as examples of black artists willing to wrestle with these inescapable themes.

By the time he wrote "The Negro Artist," Hughes had found the ideal method of tapping into the tradition that his manifesto upholds. Of his own work, Hughes says, "Most of my own poems are racial in theme and treatment, derived from the life I know. In many of them I try to grasp and hold some of the meanings and rhythms of jazz." Hughes's use of jazz and blues structures and tropes is not only the central element of his distinctive style, but also the reflection of his jazz-derived values and thought.

Some African-American writers of the 19th century, including the poet Paul Lawrence Dunbar and the prose writer Charles Waddell Chestnutt, wrote in dialect—changing the spelling of words to represent supposedly black pronunciations, and attempting to recreate the grammatical patterns attributed to mostly Southern blacks. By the Harlem Renaissance, however, dialect was recognized as an artificial construct placed on language in accordance with racial stereotypes. On the other hand, Hughes's jazz poetry operates from the starting point of a musical tradition that is original and authentic, with its own idioms and forms. One of his most well-known early poems is "The Weary Blues," which begins:

> Droning a drowsy syncopated tune,
> Rocking back and forth to a mellow croon,
>   I heard a Negro play.
> Down on Lenox Avenue the other night
> By the pale dull pallor of an old gas light
>   He did a lazy sway . . .
>   He did a lazy sway . . .
> To the tune o' those Weary Blues.
> With his ebony hands on each ivory key
> He made that poor piano moan with melody.
>   O Blues!
> Swaying to and fro on his rickety stool
> He played that sad raggy tune like a musical fool.
>   Sweet Blues!

Rhyme, alliteration, and repetition are nothing new in poetry or music, but Hughes achieves a unique effect with the variation of long and short lines, and the expostulations—"O Blues!", "Sweet Blues!"—that recall the syncopated rhythms of jazz. Those spontaneous-seeming shouts also bring to mind black spirituals and the practice of calling out in the black churches Hughes knew well. Here, then, is a volatile mixture of blues—the subject of the poem—of jazz, of spirituals, of African-American cultural practices, and the "high" culture of poetry. The poem has numerous tensions: a contemporary, local setting (it takes place on Lenox Avenue) bears the weariness caused by a long history of oppression; the pathos of the piano's "moans" competes with the comic touches of "rickety stool" and "musical fool"; and the implied religiosity of the spiritual elements vie with the secularity of the blues.

Hughes had traveled to Africa as a sailor with the merchant marine, and African music and themes were also of interest to him and to the Harlem audience he imagined. This poem is "Danse Africaine":

> The low beating of the tom-toms,
> The slow beating of the tom-toms,
>   Low . . . slow
>   Slow . . . low—
>   Stirs your blood.
>   Dance!
> A night-veiled girl
>   Whirls softly into a
>   Circle of light.
>   Whirls softly . . . slowly,
> Like a wisp of smoke around the fire—
>   And the tom-toms beat,
>   And the tom-toms beat,
> And the low beating of the tom-toms
>   Stirs your blood.

Using repetition and internal rhyme, Hughes reproduces the rhythmic effect of African drums, only to allow the syncopations of jazz to again break the surface of the poem with the surprising imperative, "Dance!".

Hughes's books of poetry include *The Weary Blues* (1926), *Fine Clothes to the Jew* (1927), *The Dream Keeper* (1932), *Shakespeare in Harlem* (1942), *Fields of Wonder* (1947), *One-Way Ticket* (1949), and *The Panther and the Lash* (published posthumously in 1967). He also selected and organized the poems in *Selected Poems of Langston Hughes* (1959). The poems in these volumes are often concerned with the mundane aspects of African-American life in Hughes's time: paying the rent, working or looking for work, drinking and gambling, encountering prejudice, laughing, singing, loving, going to church.

Hughes is particularly expert with the short lyric poem that opens outward when examined closely. Here is "Little Lyric (*Of Great Importance*)" in its entirety:

> I wish the rent
> Was heaven sent.

The seven-word poem manages to convey humor, desperation, social commentary, and a universally recognizable human wish for a divine or simply lucky respite from ceaseless cares. The single rhyme appears to have been out in the world awaiting its own discovery, so perfectly do the ideas of "rent" and "heaven sent" combine on the lips of the nameless, but all-too-familiar, speaker. As in a piece of popular music—jazz or blues—a simple rhyme is invested with "great importance" (Hughes tells us this in his title, as a blues singer would tell us by the emotion in his voice) and made to live again. Consider "Ennui":

> It's such a
> Bore
> Being always
> Poor.

Hughes often experiments with the classic blues form, which consists of a three-line stanza (Hughes breaks each line into two, making three into six); the second line repeats the first, and the third line is a response to the first two. Much of the power of a blues stanza comes from the suspense built into the arrival of the response line, whose answer may be wry, ironic, surprising, funny, or darkly true. The second stanza of "Young Gal's Blues" is sad, funny, and cruel all at once:

> I'm goin' to the po' house
> To see ma old Aunt Clew.
> Goin' to the po' house
> To see ma old Aunt Clew.
> When I'm old an' ugly
> I'll want to see somebody, too.

The speaker in "Morning After" has been drinking bad "licker" the previous night; he is sick and dreams he is in hell. But as is often the case with the blues, he can still summon a joke:

> I said, Baby! Baby!
> Please don't snore so loud.
> Baby! Please!
> Please don't snore so loud.
> You jest a little bit o' woman but you
> Sound like a great big crowd.

Hughes often rhapsodizes about this quality of the blues—"laughing to keep from crying"—and sees it as perhaps the defining attitude of the African-American experience. There is an affinity with Freud here, too, among whose central insight for the 20th century was that a joke always reveals a serious truth.

In "Morning After," the sexual politics take the form of a playful jibe; elsewhere in Hughes's poems, the relationships between men and women reflect a social milieu in which people both sustain and destroy one another. Hughes's own sexuality is an object of speculation, but like so many writers (Shakespeare in Harlem, indeed), his own feelings and opinions scatter and dematerialize before the procession of voices he overhears and ventriloquizes. The denizens of Harlem love and leave each other, but even in their most personal dealings Hughes portrays their endless negotiation of the ever-present larger community. In the "Ballad of the Girl Whose Name is Mud," the eponymous girl's reputation is ruined and her lover gone. Yet in the last stanza, we find she does not repent:

> No! The hussy's telling everybody—
> Just as though it was no sin—
> That if she had a chance
> *She'd do it agin'!*

Using the ballad—one of his favorite folk forms—Hughes sketches the kind of character he would often create in his writings: the outspoken dissenter, who refuses to acknowledge social (often racial or sexual) mores, and will not keep quiet about it.

The voices of Harlem speak the loudest in the book *Montage of a Dream Deferred* (1951), Hughes's best-known overall work. Consisting of almost 90 poems, some well known in their own right, Hughes considered the book a unified whole. His short, pithy fragments, sometimes too light-seeming in other works, take on power and significance as they reverberate and echo through the many-sided portrait of Harlem life created in the text. Hughes describes the basis for the book's forms and rhythms in a prefatory note: "In terms of current Afro-American popular music and the sources from which it has progressed—jazz, ragtime, swing, blues, boogie-woogie, and be-bop—this poem on contemporary Harlem, like be-bop, is marked by conflicting changes, sudden nuances, sharp and impudent interjections, broken rhythms, and passages sometimes in the manner of the jam session, sometimes the popular song, punctuated by the riffs, runs, breaks, and disc-tortions of the music of a community in transition." Thirty years into his career, Hughes shows himself committed to the same vision he outlined in "The Negro Artist": to draw from the well of a popular, native tradition, to chronicle and reflect upon the immediate present (including musically, since be-bop was the newest incarnation of jazz), and to wed form to content—as in the "impudent interjections" of the music, his own literary impudence, and the impudence of his many characters who are vocal about the state of African-American equality.

Montage concerns itself with the wisdom (and false wisdom) of the street, with disenfranchised children, with who wields power in a relationship, with women and men who want nothing out of a relationship but money, with the hypocrisy of America and its institutions, with the good and bad effects of World War II on Harlem, with the rent, with jazz old and new, and always with a "dream deferred." "Children's Rhymes" ends:

> *What's written down*
> *for white folks*
> *ain't for us a-tall:*
> *"Liberty and Justice—*
> *Huh—For All."*
>
> *Oop-pop-a-da!*
> *Skee! Daddle-de-do!*
> *Be-bop!*

Salt' peanuts!

De-dop!

The scat phrases (written-out sounds, like "De-dop") intrude and break up the poem just as the disbelieving "Huh" breaks the empty promise of "Liberty and Justice For All." And, just as it is necessary to sunder the smooth speaking of that promise, it is necessary to overhear the echo on the stoop in "Sister":

> *Did it ever occur to you, boy,*
> *that a woman does the best she can?*
>
> *Comment on Stoop*
> *So does a man.*

Language itself is always overheard, ricocheting off stoops and streets, deferred and deferring, reminding the squabbling residents that they must think about equality within their community just as they strive to be equal with the outside world pressing in.

Language erupts and overflows out of Harlem, too; in "Neon Signs," Hughes makes a list of the lit-up names of nightclubs and bars like "Wonder Bar," "Minton's," and "Mandalay." It was not the only time that Hughes exulted over found poetry, nor is it surprising that a poet so attuned to the music he heard would be aware, too, of other expressive artifacts. However, verbal pyrotechnics need not supply any more emphasis than the appearance of a lone three-syllable word in the midst of a prosaic oath in "Numbers":

If I ever hit for a dollar
gonna salt every dime away
in the Post Office for a rainy day.

I ain't gonna
play back a cent.

(Of course, I might
combinate *a little*
with my rent.)

As Hughes promises, his montage thrives on unexpected shifts—jokes give way to eroticism, then a sudden expression of sympathy for the Jews who have also endured a dream deferred. The shock of a poem like "Mellow" is that it could have been composed yesterday:

Into the laps
of black celebrities
white girls fall
like pale plums from a tree
beyond a high tension wall
wired for killing
which makes it
more thrilling.

By no means is this the only poem Hughes wrote that retains an uncanny relevance. What could be more lasting than the questions of the masterful "Harlem":

What happens to a dream deferred?
    Does it dry up
    like a raisin in the sun?
    Or fester like a sore—
    And then run?
    Does it stink like rotten meat?
    Or crust and sugar over—
    like a syrupy sweet?

    Maybe it just sags
    like a heavy load.

    Or does it explode?

Hughes may not have matched the pure self-expression of Whitman's "Song of Myself" in *Montage*, but he could participate in the life of his people, and let them speak for themselves, in a way that his poetic forebear could only approach from the outside.

Other notable and well-known poems by Hughes include "Jazzonia," "When Sue Wears Red," and "Brass Spittoons." "Cross" is a poem about miscegenation which Hughes called his ace-in-the-hole at poetry readings; when he read it, everybody snapped to attention again. "Mulatto" is another poem on the subject of mixed races, a theme that always fascinated Hughes. "Theme for English B," one of the poems in *Montage*, is an often-anthologized tour de force that shows Hughes playing, as well as he ever did, with the tension between questioning America and believing in its promise more than anyone. "Freedom's Plow," a longer poem lamenting the length of the road to freedom, is one among many Hughes pieces to be criticized for didacticism. But, as with "English B," the subtext of the poem can be read as an ironic challenge from Hughes, as if he were saying "Here is the supposed ideal of our nation; how will you react when I, who have known the reality of our nation, naively espouse the ideal loudest of all?" Questions of didacticism also arise regarding "Good Morning Revolution," as well as many other poems Hughes wrote when he took an interest in socialism and communism.

Two other groups of poems are particularly notable. The first is the group of "Madam" poems, concerning Madam Alberta K. Johnson, whose adventures with landlords, fortune tellers, census takers, and even death himself lead to often comic takes on one outspoken Harlem woman's day-to-day existence. Madam anticipates other recurring Hughes characters, especially Simple; analogues in modernism include Yeats's "Crazy Jane" poems.

Finally, the volume of poems entitled *Ask Your Mama* (1961) lay to rest the critique of Hughes that his language lacked complexity and did not participate in the experimental spirit of modernism. Consisting of twelve parts, *Ask Your Mama* is inspired by the African-American word game known as "the dozens," in which combatants insult one another with ever-increasing hyperbole. The poetry in *Ask Your Mama* (which is all capitalized) includes Hughes's notes for musical accompaniment and liner notes, such as would appear in a record album. The tone is often sardonic:

SANTA CLAUS, FORGIVE ME,
BUT YOUR GIFT BOOKS ARE SUBVERSIVE,
YOUR DOLLS ARE INTERRACIAL.
YOU'LL BE CALLED BY EASTLAND.

WHEN THEY ASK YOU IF YOU KNEW ME,
DON'T TAKE THE FIFTH AMENDMENT.

IN THE QUARTER OF THE NEGROES
RIDING IN A JAGUAR, SANTA CLAUS,
SEEMS LIKE ONCE I MET YOU
WITH ADAM POWELL FOR CHAUFFEUR
AND YOUR HAIR WAS BLOWING BACK
IN THE WIND.

Hughes assumes the air of a man who has been reticent for too long; all comes pouring out in a hyper-allusive carnivalesque. The imagery, loosed briefly from the bonds of Hughes's tirelessly mimetic social project, takes on an evocative surreality:

DID YOU EVER SEE TEN NEGROES
WEAVING METAL FROM TWO QUARTERS
INTO CLOTH OF DOLLARS
FOR A SUIT OF GOOD-TIME WEARING?
WEAVING OUT OF LONG-TERM CREDIT
INTEREST BEYOND CARING?

For all Hughes's commitment to formal rigor and experimentation, his short stories are more concerned with subject matter than the creation of a new aesthetic in prose. If anything, Hughes is most conversant with the telegraphic style of much modernist fiction: "It was summer. A few blocks beyond the Studevants' house, meadows and orchards and sweet fields stretched away to the far horizon. At night, stars in a velvet sky. Moon sometimes. Crickets and katydids and lightning bugs. The scent of grass, Cora waiting." The passage is from "Cora Unashamed," a story about a servant who, like so many others in Hughes, speaks up to tell the truth in the face of hypocrisy.

Many of the African-American characters in Hughes's story collection *The Ways of White Folks* (1934) are befuddled by white manners, white customs, and especially white silence. Hughes sets his stories in the South as well as the North, and tells them from the point of view of whites and blacks. In "Slave on the Block," the narration takes a wry tone to describe a white New York couple whose kind Hughes knows all too well:

They were people who went in for Negroes—Michael and Anne—the Carraways. But not in the social-service, philanthropic sort of way, no. They saw no use in helping a race that was already too charming and naive and lovely for words. Leave them unspoiled and just enjoy them, Michael and Anne felt. They went in for the Art of Negroes—the dancing that had such jungle life about it, the songs that were so simple and fervent, the poetry that was so direct, so real.

Whites and blacks misunderstand one another again and again in Hughes's fiction; comically in "Slave on the Block," and sadly in a story like "Little Dog," in which a lonely white woman is confused and dismayed by her growing love for a black janitor.

Hughes also published two other collections of stories: *Laughing to Keep from Crying* (1952) and *Something in Common and Other Stories* (1963). The stories reflect the same mix of concerns one finds in Hughes's poems. "Who's Passing for Who?" and "Something in Common" exhibit Hughes's love of farce; each ends with a punch line that elicits laughter, followed by a queasy realization of the sad truth behind the joke. "One Friday Morning" is an exercise in painful inevitability, as a young art student is promised a scholarship, then deprived of it because of her race. "Big Meeting," set at a Southern revival, contains a section of persuasive preaching reminiscent of passages in James Joyce's *A Portrait of the Artist as a Young Man* or Ralph Ellison's *Invisible Man*. "Tragedy at the Baths," a story about a love affair in Mexico, represents the strain of worldliness in Hughes's work. Hughes had traveled extensively, and sketches many vivid locales throughout his poetry and fiction. Mrs. Luella Bates Washington Jones in "Thank You, Ma'm," who captures and cooks for the boy who tries to steal her purse, brings Madam to mind. Even aspects of Hughes himself seem to make fleeting appearances—in the naive young Harlem artist in "Patron of the Arts," and the meek Chicago man who loses his mother in "On the Way Home."

Despite the success of his stories and his novel *Not Without Laughter* (1930), Hughes's prose triumph was the Simple series, which appeared regularly from 1943 to 1966 in his popular column for the Chicago *Defender*. In each installment, the character of Jess B. Semple, known as Simple, talks with a man called Boyd in a Harlem bar. Hughes describes Simple in the character notes for his play *Simply Heavenly* (1953), which was based on the Simple series: "Simple is a Chaplinesque character, slight of build, awkwardly graceful, given to flights of fancy, and positive statements of opinion—stemming from a not so positive soul . . . Simple tries hard to succeed, but the chips seldom fall just right. Yet he bounces like a rubber ball. He may go down, but he always bounds back up." Simple always brings his conversations with Boyd around to race and race-related subjects like Jim Crow, racial intermarriage, the death penalty, street violence, the legislative process, and the racism inherent in language. He comes off at first as foolish and unfairly race-obsessed, but to the intellectual Boyd's dismay, in the end Simple's satires prove sharp and indisputably germane.

Simple's tall tales, irrepressible word play, and dogged determination to talk race contrast again and again with Boyd's literality, rationality, and desire to avoid race as a problem. Simple usually begins with a whim, as in "Two Sides Not Enough":

> "What I wish is that there was different kinds of eggs, not just white eggs with a yellow eye. There ought to be blue eggs with a brown eye, and brown eggs with a blue eye, also red eggs with green eyes."
>
> "If you ever woke up and saw a red egg with a green eye on your plate, you would think you had a hang-over."
>
> "I would," said Simple. "But eggs is monotonous! No matter which side you turn an egg on, daddy-o, it is still an egg—hard on one side and soft on the other. Or, if you turn it over, it's hard on both sides. Once an egg gets in the frying pan, it has only two sides, too. And if you burn the bottom side, it comes out just like the race problem, black and white, black and white."
>
> "I thought you'd get around to race before you got through. You can't discuss any subject at all without bringing in color. God help you! And in reducing everything to two sides, as usual, you oversimplify."
>
> "What does I do?"
>
> "I say your semantics make things too simple."
>
> "My which?"
>
> "Your verbiage."
>
> "My what?"
>
> "Your words, man, your words."
>
> "Oh," said Simple. "Well, anyhow, to get back to eggs . . ."

Simple gets back to eggs just long enough to repeat that he's tired of them, just like he's tired of the race problem. The Simple series was collected in four volumes, as well as *The Best of Simple* (1961).

No overview of Hughes's work is complete without *The Big Sea* (1940) and *I Wonder as I Wander* (1956), the two autobiographical volumes that chronicle much of Hughes's remarkable life. In them, Hughes tells of his ancestry and childhood, and of people like his aunt and uncle from whom he "learned to like both Christians and sinners equally well." He describes his strong antipathy for his father, outlines his travels with the merchant marine in anecdotal fashion, and offers tantalizingly candid reflections on his writing process. Of reading, he admits, "I have no critical mind, so I usually either like a book or don't." Characteristically, Hughes reveals little about his personal relationships, yet he brings the Harlem heyday to life and populates its society parties with the greatest figures of the period. Hughes's journalistic excursion to cover the Spanish Civil War yields a convincing account of wartime atmosphere, as well as an implicit commentary on the greater freedom that a black man could enjoy in Europe at that time. Hughes is present in these volumes with all his familiar interests, whether he is memorializing the found poetry of Harlem rent-party invitations, or relating the heartbreaking tales of his own youthful confrontations with Jim Crow. The style of these books is fast moving and conversational, recalling other popular, highly readable 20th-century memoirs such as Hemingway's *A Moveable Feast* and Orwell's *Down and Out in Paris and London*.

As it does with most writers whose art aspires to social relevance, criticism on Hughes begins in controversy. Hughes could never please everyone, and sometimes pleased no one; as his biographer Arnold Rampersad once described the situation: ". . . Hughes was ceaselessly called upon to be a 'wise' person, ever vigilant as he negotiated the space between the political right and left, between the white race and the black, between the middle class who bought and read books and the poorer classes he deeply respected and wanted to reach, between the desire to speak his mind boldly and the restraint that his tenuous position demanded if he was to survive as a writer." Trapped as he was in this precarious, liminal space, forced to temper the stridency of his rhetoric if he was going to be heard at all, Hughes's ability to honor his artistic beliefs looks ever more impressive.

The reviews of Hughes's first book of poetry, *The Weary Blues*, comprise a public referendum on the mission of African-American art in general. Countee Cullen, Hughes's poet contemporary, finds in the work the "utter spontaneity and expression of a unique personality"; nevertheless, Cullen goes on to say "these poems would have been better had Mr. Hughes held himself a bit in check." Cullen's real concern soon shows itself: "Taken as a group the selections in this book seem one-sided to me. They tend to hurl this poet into the gaping pit that lies before all Negro writers, in the confines of which they become racial artists instead of artists pure and simple. There is too much emphasis here on strictly Negro themes . . ." Other Harlem literati, such as Jessie Fauset and Alain Locke, were more sympathetic to Hughes's project (which was made explicit in Hughes's "The Negro Artist" that same year), the latter proclaiming that the poems exhibit "a mystic identification with the race experience which is, I think, instinctively deeper and broader than any of our poets has yet achieved."

As Edward J. Mullen points out in his introduction to *Critical Essays on Langston Hughes*, ". . . the critical response to [Hughes's] early books involved a response to a number of subtexts in American culture: folk art versus high art, propaganda versus literature, and black art versus high art." The approach Mullen describes is obvious in the often-cited (including by Hughes himself) trio of particularly nasty barbs that greeted Hughes's sophomore volume, *Fine Clothes to the Jew*: The *Pittsburgh Courier* headline reading "Langston Hughes' Book of Poems Trash," the *New York Amsterdam*'s introduction of "Langston Hughes, the Sewer Dweller," and the *Chicago Whip*'s dubbing of Hughes as "the poet low-rate of Harlem." The African-American press panned the book on the grounds that Hughes was doing his community a disservice by portraying blacks drinking, gambling, engaging in prostitution, and living in poverty. Sherwood Anderson betrayed more insight into his own attitudes than Hughes's when he depicts the author of *The Ways of White Folks* as having "a deep-seated resentment in him. It is in his blood, so deep-seated that he seems himself unconscious of it."

Hughes's literary run-ins with the most prominent black novelists of his time—Richard Wright, Ralph Ellison, and James Baldwin—yielded mixed results. Wright, a friend, was complimentary about *The Big Sea*. Baldwin was harsh to Hughes in print; his review of *Selected Poems* begins: "Every time I read Langston Hughes I am amazed all over again by his genuine gifts and depressed that he has done so little with them," and continues, "his book contains a great deal which a more disciplined poet would have thrown into the waste-basket." Essentially, Baldwin echoes Cullen in taking the carefully crafted appearance of spontaneity in Hughes's poems as evidence of sloppiness or laziness.

For decades, as much ink was spent debating whether or not Hughes was right to adopt jazz and blues forms as on whether or not he did it well. If the question seems arbitrary—"right" or not, Hughes had made his choice—it seems less so as the debate reveals itself to be a protracted cultural discussion of the aesthetics of race. Aside from the reviews, professional criticism appeared only sporadically during Hughes lifetime, with the first major book-length study, *Langston Hughes* by James A. Emanuel, arriving in 1967—the year of Hughes's death.

In the following decades, two unofficial strains of Hughes criticism emerged. The first of these involved a serious inquiry into the relationship of Hughes's work to the African-American folk tradition he himself had sought to utilize. George E. Kent, in his essay "Hughes and the Afro-American Folk and Cultural Tradition" (1972), defines the ontological position of a tradition that includes the blues, jazz, be-bop, work songs, spirituals, gospel, sermons, and testimonials. Kent argues that the tradition recognizes the "contradictions of experience," and owns that "As a creative artist, Langston Hughes had more of an instinctive, than intellectual, sense of the folk acceptance of the contradictory as something to be borne, climbed on top of, confronted by the shrewd smile, the cynical witticism, the tragicomic scratch of the head, the tense and sucked-in bottom lip, the grim but determined look beyond this life, and, more familiarly, the howl of laughter that blacks have not yet learned to separate from the inanities of minstrel tradition." Kent's praise is clearly mediated; Hughes is not "intellectual," he is still implicated in minstrelsy. Kent's largest reservation concerns Hughes's use of the blues tradition, whose effectiveness in performance—where musician and audience meet in a unified expression—is compromised when the form is self-consciously written down as poetry. Kent opines, "Hughes is best when he attempts to capture the blues spirit and varied forms of response to existence in a poem that uses non-blues devices." Ultimately, Kent feels that Hughes's "awareness on many occasions seems more complex than the art which he can command to render it," and he points to the lack of any single masterpiece in Hughes's oeuvre as evidence of this claim.

Onwuchekwa Jemie's book, *Langston Hughes: An Introduction to the Poetry* (1976), seeks to judge Hughes's poetry on criteria derived from the African-American tradition—how can we not, Jemie argues, when jazz is a revolt against Western industrial culture itself. Jemie recognizes a "black esthetic [sic]" that includes humor, which "represents a profound criticism of America, a sane antidote to an insane circumstance," and jazz music, which Hughes "came to regard . . . as a paradigm of the black experience and a metaphor for human life in general." In the chapter "Jazz, Jive, and Jam," Jemie places jazz poetry—colloquial, exuberant, rhythmic, terse, and brisk— in opposition to the modernist aesthetic of poets like Pound and Eliot, in whose poems "the language is formal and literary, with long, complex sentences and well-made phrases, or informal but not conversational, or, when it is conversational, it is in the idiom of the educated middle class." The cultural weight enforcing the latter tradition as superior is unfortunate for a writer like Hughes, whose works are consequently judged by inappropriate standards. Jemie reads *Ask Your Mama* as a momentary capitulation to such judgments: "Compared to the electric clarity of his other books, *Ask Your Mama* is Hughes's one and only difficult book. It is his sop to academia, his answer to those readers who demand complex surfaces to puzzle over. This is the kind of poetry Hughes might have written all his life had he not had such a clear conception of his goals and of the light years of difference between formal complexity and literary worth." However, Jemie devotes most of the chapter to brilliantly mapping the associative organization of

Montage of a Dream Deferred, reveling in its multilayered orchestration and echoing Kent's observation regarding the ability of jazz forms to embrace simultaneous meanings.

In "Old John of Harlem: The Urban Folktales of Langston Hughes" (1980), the critic Susan L. Blake contends that the Simple stories best represent Hughes's appropriation of the folk tradition. Kent had detected an insuperable difference between true folk literature, which requires a shared experience between writer and audience, and self-consciously folk-like literature that yields individualized and not-necessarily shared experience. But in Blake's view, the Simple stories bridge this gap because they deal with the social conditions of a particular group in the present moment. True folk literature is not a historical object of nostalgia, but a dynamic reality, and Hughes has found the form—a humorous dialogue—as well as the vehicle— a newspaper—to convey that reality. Blake compares Simple to John, the hero of an oral tradition from the days of slavery. Just as John is a subversive figure, "Hughes's purpose in Simple's stories is to make revolution look simple."

Given Hughes's well-documented life as a public figure, his overall autobiographical candor, and his willingness to reflect openly on the creative process, it is not surprising that another strain of Hughes criticism sought to understand his work from a biographical perspective. Raymond Smith's "Hughes: Evolution of the Poetic Persona" (1974) declares, "Hughes's evolution as a poet cannot be seen apart from the circumstances of his life which thrust him into the role of a poet." For Smith, Hughes was both black and American, a Harlem resident who had grown up in the Midwest, a self-proclaimed conduit for the traditions of his race who had also traveled the world and gleaned a larger perspective. As a result of these tensions, Hughes could occupy the objective space required for true artistic expression. As the "singer," the objective artist is not entirely of his people, but is empowered to channel the expression of their hopes and cares. The result is unique: "Unlike Whitman, . . . who celebrated particular self . . . Hughes celebrated racial, rather than individual, self. Hughes tended to suppress the personal element in his poetry, appropriating the first person singular as the fitting epitome of universal human tendencies embodied in race." Hughes's "affirmation of blackness" (an idea taken up by some later critics) is his greatest asset, and Smith's intention is to chart the "process by which Hughes transformed personal experiences into archetypal racial memories." To do so, Smith often takes Hughes at his word about the author's childhood events, creative moments, and artistic principles.

Hughes's biographer Arnold Rampersad was well qualified for an investigation into his subject's life and work. Rampersad's essay "The Origins of Poetry in Langston Hughes" (1985) is initiated by the question: How did the young Hughes, who idolized Whitman and wrote poems about conventional subjects, become a poet concerned with African-American forms and experience? The piece of the puzzle initially missing is madness—the necessary element, in one form or another, of all creativity. But Rampersad realizes that madness is not absent from Hughes's life; it is only hidden behind the "image of geniality" that the poet actively promoted. This genial mask is a calculated requisite for producing the highly readable, folk-like poetry meant for the black masses that Hughes genuinely loved. Whether as a pose or an unconscious choice, the affable persona explains Hughes's mastery of the autobiographical form, which "consists in his ability to cross its chill deep by paddling nonchalantly on its surface," and it lies at the heart of the misplaced "notion that Langston Hughes was intellectually and emotionally shallow."

Rampersad discovers Hughes's madness, however deeply suppressed, in two highly emotional experiences: a bitter dispute with his father in Mexico in 1919 that ended in an illness, and another period of illness following Hughes's fallout with his patron in 1930. Of these events Rampersad observes, "Both showed a normally placid Hughes driven into deep rage by an opponent, a rage which he was unable to ventilate because the easy expression of personal anger and indignation was anathema to him." Rampersad then speculates that the creativity following these periods—the product of Hughes's suppression of anger and the heightening of his will in the heat of conflict—was in fact alien to Hughes's predisposition to *in*activity. In fact, Hughes had been relatively inactive before each incident. And this inactivity reflects the truer Hughes, the man for whom life was most akin to the oral folk poetry that relied on poetic consciousness as opposed to poetic production. Rampersad comes to an unexpected conclusion: "The notorious placidity of surface in Hughes . . . bespeaks the extent to which he was a poet who preferred his poems unwritten—a poet, like his great mentor Walt Whitman, who saw his life itself as a poem greater than any poem he could possibly write." This realization is the key to a series of further conclusions: Hughes's poetic consciousness is essentially childlike, resulting in a certain amount of vulnerability, which in turn explains periods of bleakness in Hughes's poetry and his rage in moments of abandonment, creating a psychological dependence on the black race as an eternal, protective, and balancing force in Hughes's life.

In the decades following Hughes's death, while many critics concentrated on the relation of Hughes's work to the folk tradition and to his biographical circumstances, others began to mine the less-discussed elements of the Hughes oeuvre. In "Hughes as Playwright" (1968), Darwin

T. Turner maintains that "Hughes never became outstanding as a dramatist." In his 1974 essay, Roger Rosenblatt reads the novel *Not Without Laughter* in light of both other black fiction and white bildungsroman (novels of education). Martha Cobb considers Hughes's literary fellowship with the Haitian writer Jacques Roumain and the Cuban writer Nicolás Guillén (both of whose work Hughes had translated) in her book *Harlem, Haiti, and Havana* (1979). And David Michael Nifong reads seven stories from *The Ways of White Folks*, paying attention to Hughes's narrative techniques, in an essay from 1981—the same year that the Langston Hughes Society, which publishes the *Langston Hughes Review*, was founded.

Even as Hughes criticism proliferated, the questions being asked—about the folk tradition, the "affirmation of blackness," and the function of each element in Hughes's oeuvre—remained tied to the concerns suggested by Hughes himself in works like "The Negro Artist," or to the negotiation of political positions and strategies staked out in the time of the Harlem Renaissance (i.e., the value of folk forms for a black writer). As the critic Paul Eggers complained in an essay on Hughes and Lacan, "More than forty years after the publication of *Montage*, critical treatments of the volume's poems remain confined to the interpretive field laid out by Hughes in his Introduction." Critics increasingly found that this narrow field left room for high praise or disdain, but often little in between. However, throughout the 1990s, critics began to stray from the well-worn paths of relatively straightforward Hughes criticism. Among these critics are those who, like Eggers, have applied different theoretical models to Hughes's work.

Maryemma Graham's "The Practice of a Social Art" (1990) casts Hughes as an "early radical" and considers his work from a Marxist perspective. Graham points out that Marxists in the 1920s found folk and oral traditions too susceptible to commodification, which explains the ease with which the white community was able to exploit African-American culture as a form of amusement. Nevertheless, Hughes's strong feeling for the proletarian lower classes naturally led him to a political stance antithetical to bourgeois engines of oppression. Examining the prose work in particular, Graham writes "[Hughes's] work suggested that elitist concepts of art and culture could be broken down if the artist kept before him the interests and aspirations of the masses of working-class people and an understanding of social and economic history." Graham acknowledges that Hughes was never a strident Marxist, and that his relationship to the Soviet Union was complex; still, she argues, Hughes did successfully adopt the "Marxist analytical method," and his "practice of social realism integrated the classic Marxist view of class struggle and national identity without falling victim to propagandistic phrase-mongering."

In "Heroic 'Hussies' and 'Brilliant Queers': Genderracial Resistance in the Works of Langston Hughes" (1994), Anne Borden asks what relationship exists between racial struggles in Hughes and the gender struggles faced by his characters. Of two simultaneous modes of oppression faced by an African-American woman, is it the liberation from racial or from sexual inequality that is privileged as a goal? David Jarraway also examines the many faces of Otherness in his "Montage of an Otherness Deferred: Drawing Subjectivity in Langston Hughes" (1996). Drawing on the work of critics like Henry Louis Gates, Edward Said, and Judith Butler, Jarraway locates "mystery, lack, difference, and distance" in Hughes's Harlem, where both an absence and a superfluity of meaning hold off the limitations that a state of Otherness usually imposes. By continually deferring meaning, Hughes creates the opportunity for an endlessly changing subjectivity, and thus inevitable social change. According to Jarraway, "The Otherness of deferred subjectivity in Langston Hughes's poetry suggests that an investment in any totally stable, categorizable, easily representable identity is always misplaced." No surprise, then, that Hughes deferred "stable" certitude regarding his own sexuality, or that he considered Whitman—for whom the "I" spirals ever outward—a major influence.

Finally, other critics in the last decade have sought to rethink received critical wisdom about Hughes. Karen Jackson Ford, in "Do Right to Write Right: Langston Hughes's Aesthetics of Simplicity" (1992), jokes, "The one thing most readers of twentieth-century poetry can say about Langston Hughes is that he has known rivers." Ford is referring to the repeated anthologizing of a small number of Hughes's poems that she considers uncharacteristic of his work as a whole. While supposedly "complex" poems get the attention, "The repression of the great bulk of Hughes's poems is the result of chronic critical scorn for their simplicity." But for Hughes, simplicity was a genuine aesthetic choice. The character Simple, for example, because of his simple approach, "is able to register contradictions without finally resolving them"; and "While Simple's ideas always sound regressive at first, he ultimately articulates a far more radical position than Boyd's; and he does so by rejecting the falsifying complexities Boyd raises. Boyd's willingness to view all racial issues as hopelessly intricate finally renders him ineffective and conservative. Simple's obstinacy, on the other hand, enables him to view all issues in black and white, so to speak." Ford concludes that to read Hughes properly is to value this simplicity of expression.

David Chinitz makes a similar argument in "Literacy and Authenticity: The Blues Poems of Langston Hughes" (1996). Challenging the critical commonplace that Hughes's folk-blues poems are inferior to his classic-blues poems (a distinction between original blues and later, more commercial and more polished versions of the blues), Chinitz believes that the more restrained and unfinished-seeming language of the former are ultimately more expressive. In "Jazz, Realism, and the Modernist Lyric" (2000), Anita Patterson constructs a somewhat contrary, but equally as challenging, argument for reading Hughes's poems alongside the white modernist tradition usually considered quite separate from Hughes's milieu. For Patterson, Hughes's lyric poems are "comparable to the critique of romantic cultural materialism undertaken by Ezra Pound, Hart Crane, T. S. Eliot, and other modernists writing in the aftermath of the Great War."

Patterson's recent claim reminds us that Hughes is not an isolated voice; after all, he is not far from the Harlem artist in the story "Who's Passing for Who?" who counts Gertrude Stein and *Ulysses* as required reading. But, as Ford and Chinitz suggest, we also have a responsibility to read Hughes in light of the distinct tradition to which he belonged. Hughes and his work have always lived in what W.E.B. Du Bois called a "double consciousness." Black and American, beholden to rival canons, Hughes the writer embodies the never resolved "race question" that his poems and characters would never have us forget.

WORKS CITED

Anderson, Sherwood. "Paying For Old Sins." In *Critical Essays on Langston Hughes*, ed. by Edward J. Mullen. Boston: G. K. Hall & Co., 1986.

Baldwin, James. "[Review of *Selected Poems of Langston Hughes*]." In *Langston Hughes: Critical Perspectives Past and Present*, ed. by Henry Louis Gates Jr. and K. A. Appiah. New York: Amistad, 1993.

Blake, Susan L. "Old John in Harlem: The Urban Folktales of Langston Hughes." In *Langston Hughes*, ed. by Harold Bloom. New York: Chelsea House, 1989.

Chinitz, David. "Literacy and Authenticity: The Blues Poems of Langston Hughes." *Callaloo* 19:1 (Winter 1996): 177-94.

Cullen, Countee. "Poet on Poet." In *Critical Essays on Langston Hughes*, ed. by Edward J. Mullen. Boston: G. K. Hall & Co., 1986.

Eggers, Paul. "An(other) Way to Mean: A Lacanian Reading of Langston Hughes's *Montage of a Dream Deferred*." *Studies in the Humanities* 27:1 (June 2000): 20-33.

Ford, Karen Jackson. "Do Right to Write Right: Langston Hughes's

Aesthetics of Simplicity." *Twentieth Century Literature* 38:4 (Winter 1992): 436-57.

Graham, Maryemma. "The Practice of a Social Art." In *Langston Hughes: Critical Perspectives Past and Present*, ed. by Henry Louis Gates Jr. and K. A. Appiah. New York: Amistad, 1993.

Hughes, Langston. *The Collected Poems of Langston Hughes*. New York: Vintage, 1994.

———. *The Langston Hughes Reader*. New York: George Braziller, Inc., 1958.

———. "The Negro Artist and the Racial Mountain." Reprinted in *The Langston Hughes Review* 4:1 (Spring 1985): 1-4.

Jarraway, David R. "Montage of an Otherness Deferred: Dreaming Subjectivity in Langston Hughes." *American Literature* 68:4 (December 1996): 819-38.

Jemie, Onwuchekwa. "Hughes's Black Esthetic." In *Critical Essays on Langston Hughes*, ed. by Edward J. Mullen. Boston: G. K. Hall & Co., 1986.

———. "Jazz, Jive, and Jam." In *Langston Hughes*, ed. by Harold Bloom. New York: Chelsea House, 1989.

Kent, George E. "Hughes and the Afro-American Folk and Cultural Tradition." In *Langston Hughes*, ed. by Harold Bloom. New York: Chelsea House, 1989.

Locke, Alain. "[Review of *The Weary Blues*]." In *Critical Essays on Langston Hughes*, ed. by Edward J. Mullen. Boston: G. K. Hall & Co., 1986.

Mullen, Edward J., ed. *Critical Essays on Langston Hughes*. Boston: G. K. Hall & Co., 1986.

Patterson, Anita. "Jazz, Realism, and the Modernist Lyric: The Poetry of Langston Hughes." *Modern Language Quarterly* 61:4 (December 2000): 651-82.

Rampersad, Arnold. Introduction to *I Wonder as I Wander: An Autobiographical Journey by Langston Hughes*, 2nd Hill and Wang ed. New York: Hill and Wang, 1993.

———. "The Origins of Poetry in Langston Hughes." In *Langston Hughes*, ed. by Harold Bloom. New York: Chelsea House, 1989.

Smith, Raymond. "Hughes: Evolution of the Poetic Persona." In *Langston Hughes*, ed. by Harold Bloom. New York: Chelsea House, 1989.

Turner, Darwin T. "Hughes as Playwright." In *Langston Hughes*, ed. by Harold Bloom. New York: Chelsea House, 1989.

RICHARD K. BARKSDALE

Langston Hughes: His Times and His Humanistic Techniques

In one of his critical essays, "Tradition and the Individual Talent," T. S. Eliot suggested that there is a necessary creative tension between a given tradition and most writers who choose to write in that tradition. The tradition defines an approach and a set of guidelines that tend to restrict the creativity of the individual writer, and the writer in reaction seeks to assert his independence and modify the tradition. So tradition speaks to writer and writer speaks to tradition. At times, a writer affects a given tradition little or not at all. For instance, a nineteenth-century romantic poet like Philip Freneau did not change the tradition of romantic poetry at all. On the other hand, Algernon Swinburne, because of his literary and physical encounter with sadism and various kinds of eroticism, revolted against the tradition of Victorian neoromanticism, and the tradition was never quite the same after Swinburne.

The case of Langston Hughes is not exactly comparable, but there is substantial evidence that by 1926, with the publication of his *Weary Blues*, he had broken with one or two rather well-established traditions in Afro-American literature. By no means was he alone in this act of literary insurrection; Claude McKay, Jean Toomer, and other poets of the 1920s stood with him. First, Hughes chose to modify the poetic tradition that decreed that whatever literature the Black man produced must not only protest racial conditions but promote racial integration. There was little or no place in such a literary tradition for the celebration of the Black lifestyle

From *Black American Literature and Humanism*, edited by R. Baxter Miller. © 1981 by The University of Kentucky Press. Reprinted by permission.

for its own sake. With obviously innocuous intent, Dunbar had attempted some celebration of the Black lifestyle in the post-Reconstruction rural South, but his pictures of happy pickaninnies and banjo-plucking, well-fed cabin Blacks did not square with the poverty and racial violence that seared that period. In any event, by 1920 a poetry of strong social protest which attempted to plead cultural equality with White America had become a fixed tradition in Afro-American literature. It was thought that Black America's writers could knock on the door of racial segregation and successfully plead for admission into a presumably racially integrated society. Of course, admission would not be gained unless these writers, painters, and sculptors had all been properly schooled in Western techniques and practices and thus fully qualified for acceptance. It might be pointed out in this context that to effect this end, even the so-called spirituals or sorrow-songs of the slaves were Europeanized—songs whose weird and sadly provocative melodies had had such a marked effect on northern Whites when first heard on the Carolina Sea Islands in 1862. In 1916, Harry T. Burleigh, the Black organist at New York's ultra-fashionable St. George's Episcopal Church, published his *Jubilee Songs of the United States* with every spiritual arranged so that a concert singer could sing it, "in the manner of an art song." Thus, the Black man's art in song and story was to be used primarily to promote racial acceptance and ultimately achieve racial integration. And it was clear that it had to be a Europeanized art.

Necessarily excluded from consideration in any such arrangement was the vast amount of secular folk material which had been created throughout the years of the Black man's persecution and enslavement in America. For during slavery black people had used song and story to achieve many social and political goals. They had covertly ridiculed "massa" and "missus" in song and story and had overtly expressed their disdain and hatred for the "niggah driber." And since slavery, they had sung the blues on waterfront levees and in juke joints; they had built railroads and sung about John Henry and other laboring giants; they had been on chain gangs and as prisoners had been leased out to cruel masters to cut the tall cane on the Brazos to the tune of the slashing whip and under a blazing sun which they called "Ole Hannah." They had sung as they chopped cotton on tenant farms and scrubbed and ironed clothes in the White folks' kitchens. All of this orature, as some critics have called it, was, in the opinion of certain twentieth-century monitors of Afro-American culture, to be totally excluded from common view. Innocuous tidbits might be acceptable, like James Weldon Johnson's "Since You Went Away," which was one of the "croon songs" published in his 1916 volume *Fifty Years and Other Poems*. But generally, the richly complex burden of secular folk material—the songs and stories that came out of the sweat, sorrow, and occasional joy of Black people of the lower classes—might impede integration and hence was to be expunged from the racial literary record.

The crystallization of a tradition which outlawed Black folk literature and song inevitably fostered some attitudes which adversely affected the jazz and blues which were just beginning to be established in the early 1920s when Hughes first settled in New York City. For the indictment of folk material resulted in the cultural censure of the blues singing of Bessie and Clara Smith; the jazz playing of Duke Ellington, Louis Armstrong, and Fletcher Henderson; and the song-and-dance and vaudeville showmanship of Bill Robinson, Bert Williams, Eubie Blake, and Noble Sissell. Ironically, one of the cultural monitors of the period, James Weldon Johnson, had written that the cakewalk and ragtime were two of Black America's principal contributions to American culture. Johnson had been a music man himself at one time in his career. But other strong-minded monitors of Black culture ignored Johnson and deemed that the dancing, singing, laughing, blues-singing, jazz-playing Black was too uncomfortably close to a despised folk tradition to project a proper integrationist image. In retrospect, one is forced to observe that in view of how deeply Black jazz and music have influenced both twentieth-century American and European lifestyles, this attempt to demean the image of the Black entertainer and music man of the early 1920s is indeed one of the great ironies in Afro-American cultural history.

So Langston Hughes and other young poets of the early years of the Harlem Renaissance had to confront a point of view which had quickly crystallized into a binding and restricting tradition. Hughes also developed a dislike for the tradition of racial exoticism which, largely promoted by White patrons, began to be an absorbing concern of Black writers by the mid-1920s. Although his resistance to racial exoticism eventually ruptured his relationship with his patron, Mrs. R. Osgood Mason, his fight against a tradition barring orature and the rich folk material of the lower classes of Blacks became his major struggle. The discussion to follow focuses not on how he waged a successful fight to change that tradition, but on the humanistic techniques which he used in his poetry to reflect and communicate the rich folk culture of Black people.

Before making any specific attempt to describe Hughes's use of humanistic techniques in his folk poetry, one may make at least three generalizations about his folk poetry. First, most of his folk poems have the distinctive marks of orature. They contain many instances of naming and enumerating, considerable hyperbole and understatement, and a strong infusion of street talk rhyming. Also, there is a deceptive veil of artlessness in most of the poems. Actually, there is much more art and deliberate design than one immediately perceives. I should point out in this context that Hughes prided himself on being an impromptu and impressionistic writer of poetry. His, he insisted, was not an artfully constructed poetry. But an analysis of some of his better monologues and his poems on economic and social class issues will reveal that much of his poetry was carefully and artfully crafted. The third generalization is that Hughes's folk poetry shares certain features found in other types of folk literature. There are many instances of dramatic ellipsis and narrative compression. Also, we find considerable rhythmic repetition and monosyllabic emphasis. And, of course, flooding all of his poetry is that peculiar mixture of Hughesian irony and humor—a very distinctive mark of his folk poetry.

The foregoing generalizations have a particular relevancy when one studies some of Hughes's dramatic monologues. In most instances, these are artfully done; the idioms of Black folk speech and street talk abound; and very often the final lines drip with irony and calculated understatement. An example is "Lover's Return":

> My old time daddy
> Came back home last night.
> His face was pale and
> His eyes didn't look just right.
> . . . .
> He says to me, "Mary, I'm
> Comin' home to you—
> So sick and lonesome
> I don't know what to do."

First, there are two levels of monologue in this poem; the persona describes to the reader her elderly lover's return, and then, in lines which the poet italicizes, there is an interior monologue in which the persona talks to herself. These italicized lines clearly reveal the heightened anxiety and emotional tensions that haunt her:

> *Oh, men treats women*
> *Just like a pair o' shoes.*
> *You men treats women*
> *Like a pair o' shoes—*
> *You kicks 'em round and*
> *Does 'em like you choose.*

This interior monologue contains a repressed truth, and one can imagine the tremendous psychological pressure such a repressed truth has on the psyche of the persona. Moreover, these words in the interior monologue have a double-edged relevancy; they define the persona's particular dilemma and they also effectively generalize about a larger and more universal dilemma in the arena of sexual conflict. The full psychological impact of this monologue, however, is felt in the last stanza of the poem, where the conflict between outward compassion and inner condemnation is clearly delineated:

> I looked at my daddy—
> Lawd! and I wanted to cry.
> He looked so thin—
> Lawd! that I wanted to cry.
> But de devil told me:
>   Damn a lover
>   Come home to die!

Inevitably, as the result of the carefully controlled narrative compression commonly found in the well-crafted dramatic monologue, many facts remain explicitly unstated. But Hughes calls upon the perceptive and imaginative reader to fill out the details of this miniature but poignant drama. The persona, deserted by her lover many years ago, is now forced by an obviously unfair kind of social obligation to receive him once again. Her code of faithfulness and her sense of social propriety pull her in one direction. Her sense of fair play and justice pulls her in another direction. In the end, the harassed woman is torn between a deeply instinctual desire to avoid pain and distress and a strong sense of obligation to honor an elderly lover "come home to die." Characteristically, Hughes defines the dilemma and then leaves the resolution carefully unstated. By so doing, he suggests that the vulnerable, dilemma-ridden, anti-heroic persona truly counts in the larger human equation.

Further examples of Hughes's humanistic techniques can be found in certain of his blues poems and his dialogue and debate poems. In his gutsy reaction against the tradition which censured the blues as offensive and devoid of cultural import, Hughes wrote a lot of blues poems. In fact, *Fine Clothes to the Jew* (1927), *Shakespeare in Harlem* (1942), and *One-Way Ticket* (1949) have more than their fair share of such poems. Many are uncomplicated blues statements like:

> When hard luck overtakes you
> Nothin' for you to do.
> When hard luck overtakes you
> Nothin' for you to do.

> Gather up your fine clothes
> An' sell 'em to de Jew.

or:

> I beats ma wife an'
> I beats ma side gal too.
> Beats ma wife an'
> Beats ma side gal too.
> Don't know why I do it but
> It keeps me from feelin' blue.

In these poems there is a Hughesian blend of irony and humor but no psychological complexity. One contains some advice about how to handle hard luck with minimum psychological damage; the second poem describes the casual self-acceptance of a chronic woman-beater who apparently is unaware of the extent of his problem. But in "In a Troubled Key" there is a difference. The blues form is here, but the persona is emotionally insecure:

> Still I can't help lovin' you,
> Even though you do me wrong.
> Says I can't help lovin' you
> Though you do me wrong—
> But my love might turn into a knife
> Instead of to a song.

The harassed persona is helplessly entwined in love, but there is the possibility that instead of a song of love, there will be knife-work in the night. Similarly, the blues poem "Widow Woman" has an unexpectedly ironic ending. After promising to be ever-faithful to a recently deceased "mighty lover" who had "ruled" her for "many years," in the last two lines the persona suddenly becomes aware of the full import of the freedom that is about to become hers. So the poem ends with the kind of ironic juxtaposition Hughes loved. The outwardly distraught widow stands sobbing by the open grave as she watches the grave-diggers throw dirt in her husband's face. But, inwardly, her heart soars joyfully at the prospect of freedom: ". . . you never can tell when a/Woman like me is free!"

In addition to the humanizing techniques used by Hughes in some of his dramatic monologues, the poet also sometimes presented two personae in a dramatic dialogue form of poetry. In one or two instances, the dialogue broadens into a debate which the poet humanizes by carefully illuminating the two opposing points of view. For instance, in "Sister," one of the poems in *Montage of a Dream Deferred*, a dialogue occurs between a mother and her son about his sister's involvement with a married man. The brother is embarrassed by his sister's behavior and asks: "Why don't she get a boy-friend/I can understand—some decent man?" The mother somewhat surprisingly defends her daughter; actually her Marie is the victim of the grim economic lot of the ghetto dweller. She "runs around with trash" in order to get "some cash." Thus a grim and dehumanizing economic determinism is in control of the lives of all three—the mother, the son, and the daughter. The son, however, still does not understand; he asks, "Don't decent folks have dough?" The mother, out of the wisdom of a bitter cynicism, immediately replies, "Unfortunately usually no!" And she continues: "Did it ever occur to you, boy,/that a woman does the best she can?" To this the son makes no reply, but a voice, probably the poet's, adds: "So does a man." Hughes is saying that, like the distressed, fragmented, and fallible personae of most folk poetry, human beings do the best that they can, and their failures and defeats are actually the mark of their humanity.

Another poetic dialogue, entitled "Mama and Daughter," has a slightly different thrust and meaning. There is no polarizing conflict between the two personae, but obviously each reacts quite differently to the same situation. The mother helps her daughter prepare to go "down the street" to see her "sugar sweet." As they talk, the mother becomes increasingly agitated because she remembers when she, too, went "down the street" to see her "sugar sweet." But now the romantic tinsel is gone forever from her life; her "sugar sweet" married her, got her with child, and then, like so many ghetto fathers, abandoned her to a life of unprotected loneliness. So a dramatic contrast develops between the naively hopeful daughter who is eager to join the young man she can't get off her mind, and the disillusioned mother who for different reasons can't get her errant husband off her mind. When the mother expresses the hope that her husband—"that wild young son-of-a-gun rots in hell today," her daughter replies: *Mama, Dad couldn't be still young.* The anger of the mother's final comment is the anger of all the abandoned women of all of America's urban ghettos. And what she leaves unsaid is more important than what she actually says:

> He *was* young yesterday.
> He *was* young when he—
> Turn around!
> So I can brush your back, I say!

Love and sex have tricked the mother and left her lonely and full of bitter memories, but the "down-the-street" ritual must be repeated for the daughter. Disappointment and disillusionment very probably await her later; but to Hughes disappointment and disillusionment await all lovers because these are, once again, the necessary and essential marks of the human condition.

There are three other poems by Hughes which provide interesting examples of his use of humanistic techniques. The first, "Blue Bayou," is a tersely wrought dramatic monologue in which the persona describes the circumstances leading to his death by lynching. In essence, it is an age-old southern tale of an interracial love triangle that inevitably turns out badly for the Black man. What is striking about the monologue is the poet's use of the folk symbol of the "setting sun." In some of the old blues standards, this image is a recurring motif with various overtones of meaning:

> In the evenin', in the evenin'
> When the settin' sun go down
> Ain't it lonesome, ain't it lonesome
> When your baby done left town.

or:

> Hurry sundown, hurry sundown
> See what tomorrow bring
> May bring rain
> May bring any old thing.

And at the beginning of "Blue Bayou," the "setting sun" could be a symbol of "any old thing." The persona says: "I went walkin'/By de Blue Bayou/ And I saw de sun go down." Using the narrative compression and dramatic ellipsis usually found in the folk ballad, the persona then tells his story:

> I thought about old Greeley
> And I thought about Lou
> And I saw de sun go down.
>> White man
>> Makes me work all day
>> And I works too hard
>> For too little pay—'
>> Then a White man
>> Takes my woman away.
> I'll kill old Greeley.

At this point, the persona's straight narration ends. In the next stanza, sundown as a reddening symbol of violent death is introduced, and the italicized choral chant of the lynchers is heard:

De Blue Bayou
Turns red as fire.
Put the Black man
On a rope
And pull him higher!

Then the persona returns to state with a rising crescendo of emotional stress: "I saw de sun go down."

By the time the final stanza begins, "De Blue Bayou's/A pool of fire" and the persona utters his last words:

And I saw de sun go down,
   Down,
      Down!
Lawd, I saw de sun go down.

The emphasis in this last stanza is on the word "down," used four times in the four lines, and in lines two and three "down, down!" are the only words used. And Hughes arranges the monosyllabic words so that the second literally is placed "down" from the first. Thus concludes this grim little tragedy of a triangular love affair that ended in a murder and a lynching.

Several additional critical observations may be made about this poem. First, it is interesting to note how Hughes manipulates the meaning of the setting sun. It is done with great verbal economy and tremendous dramatic finesse. At the beginning, when the persona views the setting sun, it is part of a beautiful Blue Bayou setting. But the persona's mood is blue just like the anonymous blues singer who shouts:

In the evenin', in the evenin'
When the settin' sun go down
Ain't it lonesome, ain't it lonesome
When your baby done left town.

Hughes's persona quickly and succinctly relates what has happened to his baby, Lou. We do not know whether she left voluntarily with old Greeley or had no choice. In any event, as the sun is setting, the persona decides to assert his manhood and kill old Greeley. A short time after the deed is done, the lynchers catch him by the Blue Bayou. Again the sun is setting, but now all nature begins to reflect and mirror the victim's agony. The bayou turns red with his blood; and then it becomes a pool of fire mirroring the flames that begin to burn his hanging, twisting body. Finally, the victim symbolically sees his own death as he repeats, "Lawd, I saw de sun go down." It is through his poetic technique that Hughes, the "artless" poet, conveys to the reader the brutal and agonizing slowness of the persona's death. Just as the setting sun in the American southland provides a scene of slow and lingering beauty as it sinks down, down, down over the rim of the earth, so the death of the victim is a slow and lingering agony as he sinks down, down, down into the pit of death.

It should also be stressed that, although this poem has a recurring blues motif in its use of the setting-sun image, it has a finality hardly ever found in the standard blues. In fact, all good blues reflect survival and recovery. In "Stormy Monday Blues," for instance, it takes Lou Rawls six days to get rid of his blues; then, after the "ghost walks on Friday," on Saturday he "goes out to play" and on Sunday he goes "to church to pray." In the real blues the persona is always waiting hopefully to see "what tomorrow brings." But in Hughes's "The Blue Bayou," the persona has no tomorrow. Had the poem described a tomorrow, the reader would have seen a bayou flooded with the bright colors of a beautiful sunrise; and, mirrored in the bayou's sun-flecked waters, one would see the persona's body slowly twisting in the early morning breeze. The stench of burning flesh would be everywhere and no birds would sing to greet the multi-colored dawn.

A discussion of Hughes's humanistic techniques in poetry should include two additional poems: "Jitney," an experimental poem celebrating a highly particularized mode of the Black lifestyle, and "Trumpet Player: 52nd Street," which reflects the poet's consummate artistry in one mode of genre description. Essentially, both are folk poems. "Jitney" is an exuberant salute to the jitney cabs that used to wind up and down South Parkway in Chicago and Jefferson Street in Nashville, Tennessee. They have long been supplanted by better modes of transportation, but in the 1930s and 1940s the jitneys were very much part of Black Chicago and Black Nashville.

In his poem, Hughes attempts to capture the uniqueness of the experience of riding a jitney cab on two round trips between Chicago's 31st and 63rd streets. Like the cab, the poem snakes along; each stop—31st, 35th, 47th—is a single line, thus providing the reader with the sense of movement in space. Not only does the form reflect the content in this poem; the form is the content.

The great merit of the poem is not its experimental form, however. "Jitney" is a microcosm of a moving, surging, dynamic Black Chicago. Thus the poem celebrates not so much a mode of transportation unique to Chicago's Black Southside; rather it celebrates the Southside folk who ride jitneys and hustle up and down South Parkway to go to church, to go to the market, to go to night school, to go to nightclubs and stage shows and movies. Or sometimes the time spent riding in a jitney becomes a peaceful

interlude in the hectic struggle to survive in a swiftly paced urban society—
an interlude to gossip or signify:

> Girl, ain't you heard?
> *No, Martha, I ain't heard.*
> I got a Chinese boy-friend
> Down on 43rd.
> 47th,
> 51st,
> 55th,
> 63rd,
> Martha's got a Japanese!
> Child, ain't you heard?

As people come and go, facts and circumstances obviously change; but
apparently the mood in a jitney cab is one of warm, folksy friendliness—the
kind Chicago's Black residents remembered from their "down-home" days.
Indeed, the poem suggests that in a large metropolis like Black Chicago, one
refuge from the cold anonymity of urban life is the jitney cab:

> 43rd,
> I quit Alexander!
> Honey, ain't you heard?
> 47th,
> 50th Place,
> 63rd,
> Alexander's quit Lucy!
> Baby, ain't you heard?
> . . . .
> If you want a good chicken
> You have to get there early
> And push and shove and grab!
> I'm going shopping now, child.

The pervasive mood of "Jitney," then, is one of racial exuberance and vitality.
As the cab moves up and down South Parkway, the Southside folks who jump
in and out and are busy about their business have no time to talk about
deferred dreams. Obviously, Chicago's Black citizens had as many as
Harlem's Black citizens; but the jitney provided neither the time nor the
place for in-depth discussions of racial dilemmas. It is significant that by the
time Black urban America exploded into riot and racial confrontation, the
jitneys of Chicago's South Parkway and Nashville's Jefferson Street had long
since disappeared from the urban scene.

Finally, "Trumpet Player: 52nd Street" reveals a fine blending of the best of Hughes's humanistic techniques. In the portrait of the musician we see both a particular person and a folk symbol. For Hughes, who had started writing about "long-headed jazzers" and weary blues-playing pianists back in the 1920s, regarded the black musician as a folk symbol with deep roots in the racial past. Thus in the poem's first stanza we greet the symbol, not the man. What the persona remembers, all Black musicians have remembered throughout all of slavery's troubled centuries:

> The Negro
> With the trumpet at his lips
> Has dark moons of weariness
> Beneath his eyes
> Where the smoldering memory
> Of slave ships
> Blazed to the crack of whips
> About his thighs.

The instrument he is playing has no significance; it could be a banjo, a drum, or just some bones manipulated by agile black fingers; the memory is the same. And the memory makes the music different. Etched in pain, the sound is better, the beat more impassioned, the melody more evocative. And the music flows forth with greater ease, as Dunbar's Malindy proved in "When Malindy Sings." Actually these musicians have found the "spontaneous overflow of powerful emotions" that the youthful Wordsworth was in search of and actually never found, for too often in Western artistic expression, traditional structures intervene and negate spontaneous creativity.

The poem also has its fair share of Hughesian irony. Where in ancient times man through his music sought the moon and the beautiful, ever-surging sea, now matters have changed:

> Desire
> That is longing for the moon
> Where the moonlight's but a spotlight
> In his eyes,
> Desire
> That is longing for the sea
> Where the sea's a bar-glass
> Sucker size.

So no fanciful escape from the hard facts of nightclub life is permitted. We can and must remember the past but we cannot escape the present, and through Hughes's gentle reminder one stumbles on one of history's great and o'erweening truths. If art does provide an escape from the present, it is but a temporary escape. But the memory of past pain and the awareness of the present's difficulties and deferred dreams are themes that make the *comédie humaine* so truly comic.

Finally, as the poem draws to a close, the poet presents the trumpeter himself:

> The Negro
> With the trumpet at his lips
> Whose jacket
> Has a *fine* one-button roll,
> Does not know
> Upon what riff the music slips
> Its hypodermic needle
> To his soul.

The figure of the hypodermic needle penetrating the soul of the music man suggests that the music provides only temporary relief from the difficulties of the present: jazz is a useful narcotic to allay the world's woes. But the poetic image of the hypodermic needle also suggests that jazz lovers can develop addictive personalities and become dependent on a little music that excludes the terror and woe of human existence. It is not only good for the soul but absolutely necessary for the psyche.

The final stanza of this extraordinarily well-made poem repeats what was said at the beginning of the poem about the historical role of the Black maker of music.

> But softly
> As the tunes come from his throat
> Trouble
> Mellows to a golden note.

The music anesthetizes both performer and listener against remembered pain. In fact, the 52nd Street trumpeter with his "patent-leathered" hair and his jacket with "a *fine* one-button roll" disappears from view and a folk music man of ancient origin reappears. His role has long been to convert "trouble" into beautiful music. But Hughes humanizes the function of art and music. In "Trumpet Player: 52nd Street" the poet suggests that the Black man's music nullifies the pain of the past and seals off the woe of the present. Admittedly, the poem, with its sophisticated imagery, is probably not orature of the kind found in other poems discussed above, but the Black music man described herein has long been a focal figure in producing the songs and stories that Black people have orated and sung down through the centuries.

There are many more instances of Hughes's use of humanistic techniques throughout the full range of his poetry. But this discussion has been limited to his folk poetry—to his orature. It is now clear that Hughes's devotion to this kind of poetry had two major consequences: he broke the back of a tradition which sought to exclude secular folk material from the canon of black literature. And, in his use of the language of the Black lower classes, Hughes prepared the way for the use and acceptance of the revolutionary Black street poetry of the late 1960s.

ARNOLD RAMPERSAD

The Origins of Poetry in Langston Hughes

In his study *The Life of the Poet: Beginning and Ending Poetic Careers* (1981) Lawrence Lipking asks three main questions, one of which concerns me here in the case of Langston Hughes: "How does an aspiring author of verses become a poet?" In the case of John Keats, for example, how did the poet arrive at "On First Looking into Chapman's Homer," that great leap in creative ability in which Keats, sweeping from the legend of "the realms of gold" toward modern history, "catches sight not of someone else's dream but of his own reality? He stares at his future, and surmises that he may be a poet. The sense of possibility is thrilling, the moment truly awesome. Keats has discovered Keats." Or in the well-known words of Keats himself: "The Genius of Poetry must work out its own salvation in a man: It cannot be matured by law & precept, but by sensation & watchfulness in itself—That which is creative must create itself."

Can one ask a similar question about the origins of poetry in Langston Hughes, who in June 1921, at the age of nineteen, began a celebrated career when he published his own landmark poem "The Negro Speaks of Rivers" in W. E. B. Du Bois's *Crisis* magazine? Like Keats before "Chapman's Homer," Hughes had written poems before "The Negro Speaks of Rivers." Much of the poetry before "Rivers" is available for examination, since Hughes published steadily in the monthly magazine of his high school in Cleveland, Ohio. Certain aspects of this verse are noteworthy. It has nothing

From *The Southern Review* 21, no. 3 (July 1985). © 1985 by Arnold Rampersad. Reprinted by permission.

to do with race; it is dominated by images of the poet not as a teenager but as a little child; and, in Hughes's junior year, he published his first poem in free verse, one that showed the clear influence of Walt Whitman for the first (but not the last) time. Revealing an increase in skill, Hughes's early poetry nevertheless gives no sign of a major poetic talent in the making. At some point in his development, however, something happened to Hughes that was as mysterious and as wonderful, in its own way, as the miracle that overtook John Keats after the watchful night spent with his friend Charles Cowden Clarke and a copy of Chapman's translation. With "The Negro Speaks of Rivers" the creativity in Langston Hughes, hitherto essentially unexpressed, suddenly created itself.

In writing thus about Hughes, are we taking him too seriously? With a few exceptions, literary critics have resisted offering even a modestly complicated theory concerning his creativity. His relentless affability and charm, his deep, open love of the black masses, his devotion to their folk forms, and his insistence on writing poetry that they could understand, all have contributed to the notion that Langston Hughes was intellectually and emotionally shallow. One wonders, then, at the source of the creative energy that drove him from 1921 to 1967 to write so many poems, novels, short stories, plays, operas, popular histories, children's books, and assorted other work. As a poet, Hughes virtually reinvented Afro-American poetry with his pioneering use of the blues and other folk forms; as Howard Mumford Jones marveled in a 1927 review, Hughes added the verse form of the blues to poetry in English (a form that continues to attract the best black poets, including Michael Harper, Sherley Anne Williams, and Raymond Patterson). One wonders, too, in his aspect as a poet, why this apparently happy, apparently shallow man defined his creativity in terms of unhappiness. "I felt bad for the next three or four years," he would write in *The Big Sea* about the period beginning more or less with the publication of "The Negro Speaks of Rivers," "and those were the years when I wrote most of my poetry. (For my best poems were all written when I felt the worst. When I was happy, I didn't write anything.)"

Hughes actively promoted the image of geniality to which I have alluded. Wanting and needing to be loved, he scrubbed and polished his personality until there was no abrasive side, no jagged edge that might wound another human being. Publicly and privately, his manner belied the commonly held belief that creativity and madness are allied, that neuroses and a degree of malevolence are the fair price of art. His autobiographies, *The Big Sea* (1940) and *I Wonder as I Wander* (1956), made no enemies; to many readers, Hughes's mastery of that form consists in his ability to cross its chill deep by paddling nonchalantly on its surface. And yet in two places, no doubt deliberately, Hughes allows the reader a glimpse of inner turmoil.

Both appear in the earlier book, *The Big Sea*. Both involve personal and emotional conflicts so intense that they led to physical illness. Because of their extreme rarity, as well as their strategic location in the context of his creativity, these passages deserve close scrutiny if we hope to glimpse the roots of Hughes's originality as a poet.

The first of these two illnesses took place in the summer of 1919, when Hughes (at seventeen) saw his father for the first time in a dozen years. In 1903, James Hughes had gone to Mexico, where he would become a prosperous property owner. In a lonely, impoverished, passed-around childhood in the Midwest, his son had fantasized about the man "as a kind of strong, bronze cowboy, in a big Mexican hat, going back and forth from his business in the city to his ranch in the mountains, free—in a land where there were no white folks to draw the color line, and no tenements with rent always due—just mountains and cacti: Mexico!" Elated to be invited suddenly to Mexico in 1919 at the end of his junior year in high school, Langston left the United States with high hopes for his visit.

The summer was a disaster. James Hughes proved to be an unfeeling, domineering, and materialistic man, scornful of Indians and blacks (he was himself black) and the poor in general, and contemptuous of his son's gentler pace and artistic temperament. One day, Langston could take no more: "Suddenly my stomach began to turn over and over. And I could not swallow another mouthful. Waves of heat engulfed me. My eyes burned. My body shook. I wanted more than anything on earth to hit my father, but instead I got up from the table and went back to bed. The bed went round and round and the room turned dark. Anger clotted in every vein, and my tongue tasted like dry blood." But the boy, ill for a long time, never confessed the true cause of his affliction. Having been moved to Mexico City, he declined to help his doctors: "I never told them . . . that I was sick because I hated my father." He recovered only when it was time to return to the United States.

Hughes's second major illness came eleven years later. By this time he had finished high school, returned to Mexico to live with his father for a year, attended Columbia University for one year (supported grudgingly by James Hughes), dropped out of school, and served as a messman on voyages to Africa and to Europe, where he spent several months in 1924 as a dishwasher. All the while, however, Hughes was publishing poetry in a variety of places, especially in important black journals. This activity culminated in books of verse published in 1926 (*The Weary Blues*) and 1927 (*Fine Clothes to the Jew*) that established him, with Countee Cullen, as one of two major black poets of the decade. In 1929, he graduated after three and a half years at black Lincoln University, Pennsylvania. In 1930, Hughes published his first novel, *Not without Laughter*.

This book had been virtually dragged out of him by his patron of the preceding three years, "Godmother" (as she wished to be called), an old, white, very generous but eccentric woman who ruled Hughes with a benevolent despotism inspired by her volatile beliefs in African spirituality, folk culture, mental telepathy, and the potential of his genius. But the result of her largesse was a paradox: the more comfortable he grew, the less Hughes was inclined to create. Estranged by his apparent languor, his patron finally seized on an episode of conflict to banish him once and for all. Hughes was devastated. Surviving drafts of his letters to "Godmother" reveal him deep in self-abasement before a woman with whom he was clearly in love. Ten years later, he confessed in *The Big Sea*: "I cannot write here about that last half-hour in the big bright drawing-room high above Park Avenue . . . because when I think about it, even now, something happens in the pit of my stomach that makes me ill. That beautiful room. . . suddenly became like a trap closing in, faster and faster, the room darker and darker, until the light went out with a sudden crash in the dark, and everything became like . . . that morning in Mexico when I suddenly hated my father.

"I was violently and physically ill, with my stomach turning over and over. . . . And there was no rationalizing anything. I couldn't." For several months, according to my research (Hughes erroneously presents a far briefer time frame in *The Big Sea*), he waited in excruciating hope for a reconciliation. As in Mexico, he wasted time and money on doctors without revealing to them the source of his chronic illness (which one very ingenious Harlem physician diagnosed as a Japanese tapeworm). Rather than break his silence, Hughes even agreed to have his tonsils removed. Gradually it became clear that reconciliation was impossible. Winning a prize of four hundred dollars for his novel, Hughes fled to seclusion in hot, remote Haiti. When his money ran out some months later, he returned home, healed at last but badly scarred.

Although they occurred more than a decade apart, the two illnesses were similar. Both showed a normally placid Hughes driven into deep rage by an opponent, a rage which he was unable to ventilate because the easy expression of personal anger and indignation was anathema to him. In both cases, he developed physical symptoms of hyperventilation and, eventually, anemia. More importantly, both were triggered in a period of relatively low poetic creativity (as when he was still a juvenile poet) or outright poetic inactivity (as with his patron). In each instance, Hughes had become satisfied with this low creativity or inactivity. At both times, a certain powerful figure, first his father, then "Godmother," had opposed his right to be content. His father had opposed any poetic activity at all; "Godmother" had opposed his right to enjoy the poetical state without true poetical action, or writing. In other words, a powerful will presented itself in forceful opposition to what was, in one sense, a vacuum of expressive will on Hughes's part. (Needless to say, the *apparent* absence of will in an individual can easily be a token of the presence of a very powerful will.) The result on both occasions, which was extraordinary, was first Hughes's endurance of, then his violent rebellion against, a force of will that challenged his deepest vision of the poetic life.

I use the term "will" knowing that to many people it is an obsolete concept, in spite of the revival of interest in Otto Rank, or continuing critiques of Freud's use of the term as, for example, Harold Bloom's excellent essay "Freud's Concepts of Defense and the Poetic Will." But I am referring here mainly, though not exclusively, to the will as a function of consciousness, as in the case of "Godmother's" will, or that of Hughes's father, or—far less demonstrably—Hughes's own volition. And what do I mean by Hughes's "vision of the poetic life"? I refer to what one might call unshaped or amorphous poetic consciousness, poetry not concretized or written down, but the crucial element (when combined with poetic "material") out of which written or oral poetry is made. In an old-fashioned but still significant way, the poet Richard Eberhart has written of "Will and Psyche in Poetry" (in Don Cameron Allen's *The Moment of Poetry*, 1962). Poems of the will value the body, activity, struggle, and the things of this world; poems of the psyche endorse spirit, "an uncontaminated grace," and the "elusive, passive, imaginative quality" of the world beyond this world. A poem of will, such as Marvell's "To His Coy Mistress," might involve a man calling a woman to bed; for an exemplary poem of psyche, Eberhart chose Poe's "To Helen," where desire leads directly away from sexuality toward spirit.

The notorious placidity of surface in Hughes, as I see it, bespeaks the extent to which he was a poet who preferred his poems unwritten—a poet, like his great mentor Walt Whitman, who saw his life itself as a poem greater than any poem he could possibly write. Hughes's greatest poetical instinct was to preserve his unformed or dormant poetic consciousness as the highest form of poetry. Such an instinct may suggest infantilism; one remembers Freud's unfortunate words about the link between creative writing and daydreaming. Infantilism would be wrong as an explanation. But, in Hughes's case, I suspect, the instinct had something to do with the youthfulness of the self he clearly regarded as his authentic, or most cherished self. Placidity of surface, anxiety to please and to be loved, apparent asexuality (the most consistent conclusion—rather than that of homosexuality, for which there is no evidence—about his libido among people who knew him well), and the compulsion against concretized or written poetry reflect a sense of self as prepubescent, or apubescent; in other words, a sense of self as an eternal child. At some level, Hughes saw himself ideally as a child—a dreamy genius child, a perfect child, a princely child, a loving child, even a mothering and maternal child—but first and foremost as a child (almost never is he the destructively rebellious child, in spite of his radical poetry).

It must be stressed that such a sense of self, although it modulates art (as does every other factor of comparable importance), is by no means an inherent handicap to a creative person. In any event, Hughes teetered between a sense of confidence (a sense of being loved by a particular person to whom he was emotionally mortgaged) and a rival, harrowing sense, born in his own childhood, of abandonment and despair. The latter was closer to the origins of his poetry. Release Hughes as an artist from the stabilizing social context and he flies almost immediately toward themes of nihilism and death. For example, take his poem "Border Line":

> I used to wonder
> About living and dying—
> I think the difference lies
> Between tears and crying.
>
> I used to wonder
> About here and there—
> I think the distance
> Is nowhere.

Or "Genius Child":

> *. . . Nobody loves a genius child.*
>
> Can you love an eagle,
> Tame or wild?
>
> Wild or tame,
> Can you love a monster
> Of frightening name?
>
> *Nobody loves a genius child.*
>
> *Kill him*—and let his soul run wild!

Or "End":

There are
No clocks on the wall,
And no time,
No shadows that move
From dawn to dusk
Across the floor.

There is neither light
Nor dark
Outside the door.

There is no door!

In Hughes's writing, there is precious little middle ground between such verse and that for which he is far better known (and deservedly so), the poems steeped in race and other social concerns. Nature as flora and fauna bored the man who preferred Harlem in hot summer to the cool New England woods, as he once joked, because "I prefer wild people to wild animals." Hughes understood wherein his salvation rested.

This bleakness, almost always ignored in critical treatments of Hughes, evolved out of the saturation of his dormant poetical consciousness by the powerful will toward death stimulated in him by his loneliness as a child. But Hughes did not surrender passively to the force of his father and "Godmother" when they turned against him. These attacks, in fact, elicited in him a massive retaliatory display of willfulness, at first (while he was ill) as uncontrolled and uncontrollable as the right to the passive poetic consciousness it defended. The invocation of will in such massive degree could easily have remained as toxic as it was while he was sick with his silent rage. Only the modification of will, a compromise between passive poetic consciousness and the purposefulness needed to defend that consciousness, could prevent the consummation of poetry (amorphous or concrete) by rage. And only an appeal to a third force that was neither Hughes nor his enemy could allow him to fashion a balance between will and his unformed poetical consciousness.

Both in the experience with his father in Mexico and in the struggle with "Godmother," the third force was represented by the black race. Hughes's attitude to the black masses is too complicated to detail here. But my argument depends on the crucial understanding that Hughes was virtually unique among major black writers not so much because of the considerable depth of his love of black people, but because of *the depth of his psychological dependence on them.* Hughes became dependent because of a

relatively complicated set of circumstances in his youth, when he was reared
by his poor but very proud grandmother, the aged, wrinkled, and laconic
Mary Langston, whose first husband had died at Harpers Ferry with John
Brown. But Mary Langston's zeal to defend the rights of her race was offset
for her grandson by her personal remoteness both from him and the race,
and by the severity of her pride—a pride compounded by her very light skin,
her Indian rather than predominantly African features, her Oberlin
education, and her high-toned religion, which all kept her distant from the
black masses. She did not attend black churches, did not sing black spirituals
(much less the blues); she spoke in a clipped manner, rather than a folksy
drawl, and she detested popular culture—as Hughes spelled out partially in
The Big Sea, but more completely in an unpublished portrait prepared in
1943.

What Mary Langston offered in the abstract, however, was made
wonderfully concrete to young Hughes by two persons with whom he lived
from time to time (when his grandmother was forced to rent out her house,
and after she died) and whom he described in an Arcadian paragraph in *The
Big Sea*—"Uncle" and "Auntie" Reed. "Uncle" James Reed, who dug ditches
for the city, smoked his pipe and stayed home on Sundays. "Auntie" Reed
(later Mrs. Mary J. Reed Campbell) took Langston to St. Luke's A.M.E.
church (a church apparently not good enough for his grandmother) and
taught the Sunday School there in which the boy was the brightest star.
Through the childless Reeds, who clearly adored the boy, he learned how to
love the race, its church ways and folk ways, and its dreams and aspirations,
of which the handsome, scrubbed, light brown boy, the grandson of
"Colonel" Charles Langston (whose brother John Mercer Langston had
served in the U.S. Congress and as an ambassador of the United States) was
the shining embodiment. And it was a lie he told to the Reeds (that Jesus had
come to Hughes at a revival meeting, after "Auntie" Reed had prayed that
this would happen) that led to the major trauma of his childhood, as related
in *The Big Sea*—a long weeping into the night (the second to last time he
cried, Hughes wrote) because he had waited for Jesus, who had never come,
then had lied to the people who loved him most. In *The Big Sea* Hughes
would admit to hating his father; he would partly ridicule his mother; he
would admit that he did not cry when his grandmother died. The Reeds,
however, were different: "For me, there have never been any better people in
the world. I loved them very much."

In his bitter struggles with his father and "Godmother," Hughes turned
to the black race for direction. But one needs to remember that this appeal
in itself hardly gave Hughes distinction as a poet; what made Hughes distinct
was the highly original manner in which he internalized the Afro-American
racial dilemma and expressed it in poems such as "When Sue Wears Red,"
"The Negro Speaks of Rivers," "Mother to Son," "Dream Variations," and

"The Weary Blues," poems of Hughes's young manhood on which his career would rest. Of these, the most important was "The Negro Speaks of Rivers."

> I've known rivers.
> I've known rivers ancient as the world and older
>   than the flow of human blood in human veins.
>
> My soul has grown deep like the rivers.
>
> I bathed in the Euphrates when dawns were young.
> I built my hut near the Congo and it lulled me to sleep.
> I looked upon the Nile and raised the pyramids above it.
> I heard the singing of the Mississippi when Abe Lincoln
>   went down to New Orleans, and I've seen its muddy
>   bosom turn all golden in the sunset.
>
> I've known rivers:
> Ancient, dusky rivers.
>
> My soul has grown deep like the rivers.

Here, the persona moves steadily from dimly starred personal memory ("I've known rivers") toward a rendezvous with modern history (Lincoln going down the Mississippi and seeing the horror of slavery that, according to legend, would make him one day free the slaves). The death wish, benign but suffusing, of its images of rivers older than human blood, of souls grown as deep as these rivers, gives way steadily to an altering, ennobling vision whose final effect gleams in the evocation of the Mississippi's "muddy bosom" turning at last "all golden in the sunset." Personal anguish has been alchemized by the poet into a gracious meditation on his race, whose despised ("muddy") culture and history, irradiated by the poet's vision, changes within the poem from mud into gold. This is a classic example of the essential process of creativity in Hughes.

The poem came to him, according to Hughes (accurately, it seems clear) about ten months after his Mexican illness, when he was riding a train from Cleveland to Mexico to rejoin his father. The time was sundown, the place the Mississippi outside St. Louis. "All day on the train I had been thinking of my father," he would write in *The Big Sea*. "Now it was just sunset and we crossed the Mississippi, slowly, over a long bridge. I looked out of the window of the Pullman at the great muddy river flowing down toward the heart of the South, and I began to think what that river, the old Mississippi, had meant to Negroes in the past—how to be sold down the river was the worst fate that could overtake a slave in bondage. Then I remembered reading how Abraham Lincoln had made a trip down the Mississippi on a raft, and how he had seen slavery at its worst, and had decided within himself that it should be removed from American life. Then I began to think of other rivers in our past—the Congo, and the Niger, and the Nile in Africa—and the thought came to me: 'I've known rivers,' and I put it down on the back of an envelope I had in my pocket, and within the space of ten or fifteen minutes, as the train gathered speed in the dusk, I had written this poem."

Here, starting with anguish over his father, Hughes discovered the compressed ritual of passivity, challenge, turmoil, and transcendence he would probably have to re-create, doubtless in variant forms, during the great poetic trysts of his life. Even after he became a successful, published poet, the basic process remained the same, because his psychology remained largely the same even though he had become technically expert. In his second major illness, caused by his patron "Godmother," Hughes wrote poetry as he struggled for a transcendence that would be long in coming. The nature of that interim poetry is telling. When he sent some poems to a friend for a little book to be printed privately, she noticed at once that many spoke of death—"Dear lovely Death/That taketh all things under wing—/Never to kill. . . ." She called the booklet *Dear Lovely Death*. In "Afro-American Fragment," unlike in "The Negro Speaks of Rivers," Africa is seen plaintively:

> . . . Subdued and time-lost
> Are the drums—and yet
> Through some vast mist of race
> There comes this song
> I do not understand,
> This song of atavistic land,
> Of bitter yearnings lost
> Without a place—
> So long,
> So far away
> Is Africa's
> Dark face.

But when Hughes returned home, scarred but healed, after months in seclusion in Haiti, he no longer thought of loss and death. Instead, he plunged directly into the life of the black masses with a seven-month tour of the South in which he read his poetry in their churches and schools. Then he set out for the Soviet Union, where he would spend more than a year.

Hughes then reached the zenith of his revolutionary ardor with poems (or verse) such as "Good Morning Revolution," "Goodbye Christ," and "Put One More 'S' in the USA."

"Good Morning Revolution," for example, and "The Negro Speaks of Rivers" are very different poems. The former is the polar opposite of the poetry of nihilism; the latter blends aspects of existential gloom with the life-affirming spirit of the black race. Together, the poems illustrate the wide range of possibility in the mixture of will and passivity which characterizes Hughes's art (although one can argue that "Good Morning Revolution"—by far the lesser poem—marks an overreaction of will, and thus is not truly representative of Hughes's poetic temperament in that it contains no element of passivity). But the creative process has remained the same. The right to amorphous poetic consciousness is challenged. The will is aroused in defense of that consciousness. Illness (an extreme version of Wallace Stevens's "blessed rage for order"?) marks the struggle of will against opposing will. The long-endured illness, in silence, gradually allows the mutual fertilization of will and poetic consciousness that is needed for concrete art. Illness ends when that ratio is achieved or perceived, and writing begins. Creativity, in Keats's term, has created itself. A poet, or a poem, is born.

To some extent, this process is nothing more than Wordsworth's definition of poetry as the final recollection "in tranquility" (a phrase often underplayed or even ignored in quoting Wordsworth's definition) of emotion that had once spontaneously overflowed. What is different, of course, is that Wordsworth (and Keats and Stevens) did not have to contend with race as a factor in his creativity. For many writers, perhaps even most, race is a distracting, demoralizing force. Hughes's genius, or his good fortune, consisted in his ability to accommodate race harmoniously within the scheme of creativity common to all major poets, and to turn it from an anomaly into an intimate advantage.

KAREN JACKSON FORD

Do Right to Write Right:
Langston Hughes's Aesthetics of Simplicity

The one thing most readers of twentieth-century American poetry can say about Langston Hughes is that he has known rivers. "The Negro Speaks of Rivers" has become memorable for its lofty, oratorical tone, mythic scope, and powerful rhythmic repetitions:

> I've known rivers:
> I've known rivers ancient as the world and older than
> the flow of human blood in human veins.

(1656)

But however beautiful its cadences, the poem is remembered primarily because it is Hughes's most frequently anthologized work. The fact is, "The Negro Speaks of Rivers" is one of Hughes's most uncharacteristic poems, and yet it has defined his reputation, along with a small but constant selection of other poems included in anthologies. "A Negro Speaks of Rivers," "A House in Taos," "The Weary Blues," "Montage of a Dream Deferred," "Theme for English B," "Refugee in America," and "I, Too"—these poems invariably comprise his anthology repertoire despite the fact that none of them typifies his writing. What makes these poems atypical is exactly what makes them appealing and intelligible to the scholars who edit anthologies— their complexity. True, anthologies produced in the current market, which is hospitable to the African-American tradition and to canon reform, now

From *Twentieth Century Literature* 38, no. 4, (Winter 1992). © 1992 by Hofstra University. Reprinted by permission.

include a brief selection of poems in black folk forms. But even though Hughes has fared better in anthologies than most African-American writers, only a small and predictable segment of his poetry has been preserved. A look back through the original volumes of poetry, and even through the severely redrawn *Selected Poems*, reveals a wealth of simpler poems we ought to be reading.[1]

Admittedly, an account of Hughes's poetic simplicity requires some qualification. Most obvious is the fact that he wrote poems that are not simple. "A Negro Speaks of Rivers" is oracular; "The Weary Blues" concludes enigmatically; "A House in Taos" is classically modernist in both its fragmented form and its decadent sensibility. Even more to the point, many of the poems that have been deemed simple are only ironically so. "The Black Christ," for example, is a little jingle that invokes monstrous cultural complexity. Likewise, two later books, *Ask Your Mama* (1961) and *The Panther and the Lash* (1967), contain an intricate vision of American history beneath their simple surfaces.[2] Nevertheless, the overwhelming proportion of poems in the Hughes canon consists of work in the simpler style; and even those poems that can yield complexities make use of simplicity in ways that ought not to be ignored.

The repression of the great bulk of Hughes's poems is the result of chronic critical scorn for their simplicity. Throughout his long career, but especially after his first two volumes of poetry (readers were at first willing to assume that a youthful poet might grow to be more complex), his books received their harshest reviews for a variety of "flaws" that all originate in an aesthetics of simplicity. From his first book, *The Weary Blues* (1926), to his last one, *The Panther and the Lash* (1967), the reviews invoke a litany of faults: the poems are superficial, infantile, silly, small, unpoetic, common, jejune, iterative, and, of course, simple.[3] Even his admirers reluctantly conclude that Hughes's poetics failed. Saunders Redding flatly opposes simplicity and artfulness: "While Hughes's rejection of his own growth shows an admirable loyalty to his self-commitment as the poet of the 'simple, Negro commonfolk' . . . it does a disservice to his art" (Mullen 74). James Baldwin, who recognizes the potential of simplicity as an artistic principle, faults the poems for "tak[ing] refuge . . . in a fake simplicity in order to avoid the very difficult simplicity of the experience" (Mullen 85).

Despite a lifetime of critical disappointments, then, Hughes remained loyal to the aesthetic program he had outlined in 1926 in his decisive poetic treatise, "The Negro Artist and the Racial Mountain." There he had predicted that the common people would "give to this world its truly great Negro artist, the one who is not afraid to be himself," a poet who would explore the "great field of unused [folk] material ready for his art" and recognize that this source would provide "sufficient matter to furnish a black artist with a lifetime of creative work" (692). This is clearly a portrait of the poet Hughes would become, and he maintained his fidelity to this ideal at great cost to his literary reputation.

In what follows I will look at some of that forgotten poetry and propose a way to read it that refutes the criticism that most of Hughes's poetry is too simple for serious consideration. I will first reconstruct Hughes's conception of the poet by looking at one of his prose characters who embodies his poetics; and, second, I will turn to a reading of *Shakespeare in Harlem* (1942), a volume of poetry that typifies Hughes's aesthetic program.

In his column in the *Chicago Defender* on February 13, 1943, Hughes first introduced the prototype of the humorous and beloved fictional character Jesse B. Semple, nicknamed by his Harlem friends "Simple." For the next twenty-three years Hughes would continue to publish Simple stories both in the *Defender* and in several volumes of collected and edited pieces.[4] Hughes called Simple his "ace-boy," and it is surely not coincidental that the Simple stories span the years, the 1940s to the 1960s, when Langston Hughes needed a literary ace in the hole.[5] The success of the Simple stories was an important consolation of the writer's later years, when his poetry was reviewed with disappointment, his autobiography dismissed as "chit-chat," his plays refused on Broadway, and his fiction diminished in importance next to Richard Wright's *Native Son* (1940) and Ralph Ellison's *Invisible Man* (1952).[6]

It seems obvious, however, that in the long association with his ace-boy Hughes found more than popularity and financial success. In fact, his prefatory sketches of Simple attest to the character's importance, in the sheer number of times Hughes sets out to explain him and in the specific details these explanations provide.[7] All of them depict Simple as an African American Everyman, the authentic—even unmediated—voice of the community that engendered him. For instance, in "Who Is Simple?" Hughes emphasizes the authenticity of his creation: "[Simple's] first words came directly out of the mouth of a young man who lived just down the block from me" (*Best* vii). Here and elsewhere Hughes asserts a vital connection between the fictional character and the people he represents: "If there were not a lot of genial souls in Harlem as talkative as Simple, I would never have these tales to write down that are 'just like him'" (*Best* viii). The author's dedication to Simple is surely rooted in his conviction that Simple embodies and speaks for the very people to whom Hughes had committed himself back in the 1920s. But Hughes's affinity with Simple is more complete than this.

Commentators on the Simple stories have concentrated on two points: theme, "Hughes's handling of the race issue" (Mullen 20); and genre, "the generic nature of these prose sketches" Mullen 20).[8] It is exclusively Hughes as prose artist we have acknowledged when considering these tales. However, I will argue that the Simple stories reveal a great deal about Hughes's poetic genius as well. Casting Simple as the figure of the poet illuminates Hughes's poetic program and explains his powerful affinity with his prose creation.

Crucial in tracing Simple's significance are the "Character Notes" to the 1957 musical comedy *Simply Heavenly*, which describe Simple in terms that stress his contradictions:

> Simple is a Chaplinesque character, slight of build, awkwardly graceful, given to flights of fancy, and positive statements of opinion—stemming from a not so positive soul. He is dark with a likable smile, ordinarily dressed, except for rather flamboyant summer sports shirts. Simple tries hard to succeed, but the chips seldom fall just right. Yet he bounces like a rubber ball. He may go down, but he always bounds back up.   (*Plays* 115)

The parallel to Charlie Chaplin, an icon of contradiction, is telling. Like Chaplin, whose physical appearance announces internal tensions (his hat is too small, his shoes too large, his vest too tight, his pants too loose), Simple is awkward yet graceful, ordinary yet flamboyant. And, again as with Chaplin, these external tensions reveal deeper ones; he is obstinate yet fanciful, decent yet flawed, and—perhaps most poignant for Hughes—optimistic despite failure.

Simple is a compelling figure for Hughes precisely because of these tensions. For these contraries—even the apparently internal ones—hang about Simple like a fool's motley. The fool's motley, of course, traditionally implies chaos; yet while his multicolored costume reflects the intricacies and contradictions around him, the fool himself may often be a perfect simpleton. This is also true of Hughes's character: though his appearance and even to some extent his character express contradiction, his fundamental nature is unequivocally simple. Obstinate, positivistic, and optimistic, Simple is able to register contradictions without finally resolving them and therefore has special significance for Hughes's poetic project. Hughes, after all, claims that "where life is simple, truth and reality are one" (*Big Sea* 311). Yet where in America is life simple for African Americans? The "where" Hughes invokes is not a place but a state of mind. The terms of his formulation—simplicity, truth, reality—are broad and vague because they are nearly synonymous to him. If one recognizes the simple facts of life, one will be able to see the truth; if one lives by the truth, one's reality will match one's ideals. Simplicity *is* truth in Hughes's vision.

Simple is the personification of such a poetics, a philosophy of composition that resorts to simplicity, not in response to singleness or triviality, but, ironically, in response to almost unspeakable contradiction. This is why he appears surrounded by complexities—his culture, his friends, even his clothing registering the confusion of the world around him. To shift the metaphor, simpleness, in both the character and the poetry, functions as a brick wall against which complexities collide. In its artless, uncomprehending refusal to incorporate contradictions, it exacerbates them. For a poet who equates simplicity with truth, cultivating a thematics and aesthetics of simplicity is essential—poetically and politically. Simplicity resists the pernicious subtleties and complexities of integrationist thought. Further, it reveals the inadequacies of such thought. But more important, it achieves these aims by reinstating the truth.

Let me turn to some examples. In "There Ought to Be a Law," Simple tells his friend Boyd that Congress ought to pass a law "setting up a few Game Preserves for Negroes" (*Reader* 181). Having seen a short movie about wildlife preserves, where "buffaloes roam and nobody can shoot a single one of them" (181), Simple concludes that "Congress ought to set aside some place where we can go and nobody can jump on us and beat us, neither lynch us nor Jim Crow us every day. Colored folks rate as much protection as a buffalo, or a deer" (181). Boyd, Simple's educated integrationist foil, first faults the plan for drawing a parallel between animals and humans: "Negroes are not wild," he asserts confidently. Yet in observing Simple's logical flaw, he misses Simple's important point. Precisely because blacks are human beings, they should be treated better than animals. Boyd admits, "You have a point there" (181), but immediately discerns another shortcoming in Simple's argument. When Simple says that one of the things he would like about living on a preserve is that he could "fight in peace and not get fined them high fines" (182), Boyd recoils: "You disgust me. I thought you were talking about a place where you could be quiet and compose your mind" (182). Again Boyd reacts against the racist stereotype that black men are physically aggressive.

In fact, however, the freedom to fight was suggested to Simple by a scene in the movie showing two elks locking horns. While Boyd would replace one behavioral cliché (black men fighting) with another (men meditating in nature), he fails to see that both prescriptions curtail freedom. Once again, Simple makes the more substantial point: "I would like a place where I could do both" (182). While Simple's ideas always sound regressive at first, he ultimately articulates a far more radical position than Boyd's; and he does so by rejecting the falsifying complexities Boyd raises. Boyd's willingness to view all racial issues as hopelessly intricate finally renders him ineffective and conservative. Simple's obstinacy, on the other hand, enables him to view all issues in black and white, so to speak. Indeed, "There Ought to Be a Law" introduces, in a back-handed way, a black separatist position that Simple holds throughout the stories. Far from capitulating to white racist stereotypes about African Americans, Simple advocates a complete break with the white world and, thus, a thorough rejection of white racist assumptions.⁹

When Simple tries his hand at poetry in two stories, we can begin to see how he embodies Hughes's conception of the poet. Ironically, in "Wooing the Muse" Simple is first inspired to compose poetry when he leaves the city to spend his vacation on the beach. Though the natural setting is a conventional pretext for poetry, Simple's verses ignore the romantic idealization of nature in favor of his characteristic realism regarding a subject that interests him more, human nature:

> Sitting under the trees
> With the birds and the bees
> Watching the girls go by.   (*Best* 28)

In fact, he gently mocks Romantic clichés like "the birds and the bees" by incorporating such phrases into his irreverent lines. But it is precisely their status as clichés that Simple exploits, tossing off such lines as empty gestures toward figuration to contrast the way his poems barrel unmetaphorically toward their artless points (though his prose is highly figurative). And, of course, that second line is not just any cliché but a euphemism for sexual relations, and thus it receives a double reproof when Simple follows it with his blunt restatement, "Watching the girls go by."

Predictably, Boyd misses the poem's own logic and faults the verse for its failure to realize conventional Anglo-American form: "You ought to have another rhyme. *By* ought to rhyme with *sky* or something" (28). Boyd cannot read the poem on its own terms but views it only as an unfinished quatrain composed (ideally) of two rhymed (aa/bb) couplets. Simple, on the other hand, sees no reason why form should exceed meaning: "I was not looking at no sky, as I told you in the poem. I was looking at the girls" (30).

Simple's second poem is a free-verse composition about racism; "This next one is a killer," he tells Boyd. "It's serious" (30). In it he compares the treatment of non-black immigrants in the United States with the mistreatment of African Americans:

> I wonder how it can be
> That Greeks, Germans, Jews,

Italians, Mexicans,
And everybody but me
Down South can ride in the trains,
Streetcars and busses
Without any fusses.
But when I come along—
Pure American—
They got a sign up
For me to ride behind:
    COLORED
My folks and my folks' folkses
And their folkses before
Have been here 300 years or more—
Yet any foreigner from Polish to Dutch
Rides anywhere he want to
And is not subject to such
Treatments as my fellow-men give me
In this Land of the Free.   (30)

Again the poem is evaluated in terms of conventional literary standards when Joyce, Simple's fiancée, wants him "to change *folkses* to say *peoples*" in order to elevate its diction (31). But since Simple doesn't have an eraser, his original phrasing is preserved. This suggests another constituent feature of Simple's poetry: it is improvisational. Even when he writes poems, they are subject to the pressures of the immediate moment and cannot be polished or refined.

While the lack of an eraser might suggest the opposite, that the poem is fixed and unchangeable, it actually indicates that the process of composition—rather than the product (which is another matter and might receive revision at another time)—is spontaneous and improvisational. In fact, Simple thinks this poem should be longer, but he has to conclude it where he does because Joyce interrupts him during composition. And his sense that the poem should have been longer derives not from some external formal measure but from the integral relationship of structure and meaning. Boyd, on the other hand, thinks "It's long enough" because he doubts the poem's worth; but Simple asserts, "It's not as long as Jim Crow" (31).

After a lengthy discussion with Boyd about why he does not write more nature poems, Simple recites a third piece—a ten-stanza toast in the "counting rhymes" genre, structured in tercets (until the final stanza which is five lines) rhyming aab, like a blues stanza. The "b" line in each stanza is also a refrain line throughout, as in a ballad:

> When I get to be ninety-one
> And my running days is done,
> Then I will do better.   (33)

Simple has concocted this toast as a retort to people who tell him, as Boyd has just done, "You should be old enough to know better." Simple distinguishes between "knowing" and "doing":

> "I might be old enough to know better, but I am not old enough to *do* better," said Simple. "Come on in the bar and I will say you a toast I made up the last time somebody told me just what you are saying now about doing better. . . . That's right bartender, two beers for two steers. . . . Thank you! . . . Pay for them, chum! . . . Now, here goes. Listen fluently."   (33)

Several points in this passage bear upon Simple's poetic practice. Most important is the assertion that recognizing (knowing) social or literary conventions need not result in enacting them (doing). When Simple orders "two beers for two steers," he playfully supports this by infusing the poetical (by virtue of the rhymes) into the mundane as easily as he has infused the mundane into the poetical. Finally, when Simple cautions Boyd to "Listen fluently," he coins a phrase that will appear again and again in the stories, whenever Simple suspects that habitual ways of "reading" will obstruct the proper reception of his compositions. The odd phrase pulls artist and audience together, insisting that writer and reader accompany each other in a new literacy. "Listen fluently" also introduces orality, and appropriately so, since it precedes the toast, an oral composition, and thus widens the scope of poetry. As we have seen, many of Simple's poetic models are African-American folk forms—ballads, blues, toasts—genres that can claim written *and* oral status. Certainly Hughes, like Simple, "knows" about literary convention but chooses to "do" things his own way.

The opposition of correctness as knowledge and correctness as action (in the context of poetry, "action" means writing truthfully) is central to "Grammar and Goodness," another story that treats Simple's poetic production. Simple's formulation of this borders on the nonsensical, like many of his wise sayings: "It is better to *do* right than to write right" (*Stakes* 182). Simple reads two poems to the narrator (who in this story is apparently not Boyd). The first is one that Joyce and Boyd have edited. Its conclusion uneasily renders Boyd's accommodationist perspective in Simple's belligerent style:

Now, listen, white folks:
In line with Rev. King
Down in Montgomery—
Also because the Bible
Says I must—
In spite of bombs and buses,
I'm gonna love you.
I say, I'm gonna LOVE you—
White folks, OR BUST!   (181)

The "authorities"—Reverend King and the Bible (and behind them, certainly, Joyce and Boyd)—want Simple's poem to advocate loving the enemy.

However, this conciliatory theme is gainsaid by the imperative construction, the screaming capital letters, the allusions to white violence, and the threatening last line (which comes off as a warning to whites to *be* lovable rather than as a promise on Simple's part to love them "in spite" of themselves). Despite these obvious contradictions, the narrator extricates a coherent "message" from the piece by ignoring its style, and doubts whether Simple could have written such a poem: "You never wrote a poem that logical all by yourself in life" (181). Simple admits this freely and offers another, unedited, poem in its place; it is no surprise when it completely contradicts the first one. It begins,

In the North
The Jim Crow line
Ain't clear—
But it's here!

and ends,

Up North Jim Crow
Wears an angel's grin—
But still he sin.
I swear he do!
Don't you?   (181)

Though the narrator agrees with the sentiment of this poem, he chides Simple "for the grammar" (182). Simple once again rejects the notion that poems must meet formal standards, claiming, "If I get the sense right . . . the grammar can take care of itself" (182). Both "Wooing the Muse" and

"Grammar and Goodness" repudiate the aesthetics of traditional poetry, especially adherence to conventional forms, elevation of diction, preference for written rather than oral forms, the necessity of polish and finish, and the subordination of content to form.

Simple is thus a folk poet in the African and African-American traditions. His poems are communal, colloquial, and often improvisational. When he uses existing verse forms, he chooses ballads, blues, toasts, and spirituals. Moreover, his speech is rendered lyrical through a high content of figuration and internal rhyme.[10] In addition to his status as folk poet, however, Simple is the embodiment of—and, considering his life span, perhaps the defender of—Langston Hughes's aesthetic program. His name, an epigrammatic poem in its own right, captures this aspect of the character. In "Family History" Simple explains his highly suggestive name:

> "Grandpa's name was Jess, too. So I am Jesse B. Semple."
> "What does the *B* stand for?"
> "Nothing. I just put it there myself since they didn't give me
> no initial when I was born. I am really Jess Semple."
>
> (*Speaks* 179)

Simple's name invokes his family history, a heritage that the story reveals is multi-racial. His name, then, links him to a diverse cultural past and thereby at least superficially legitimates him as a representative figure. A second interesting feature of his name is the self-defining middle initial "B." He says the "B" stands for nothing, but knowing him, we wonder if it doesn't signify "black." Or, it may derive from another story, "Bop," in which he explains to Boyd that the difference between the prefixes "*Re* and *Be*" (in "Re-Bop" and "Be-Bop") is that the "Be" signifies "the real thing like the colored boys play" (*Wife* 56). In such a reading, the middle initial "B" might indicate the integrity of self-authorship, a prerequisite for being an authentic representative of his larger culture. Even more suggestive are the puns involved in Simple's names. By giving himself the middle initial he transforms his given name from a negative description of himself—Jess Semple ("just simple")—into an imperative statement—Jess B. Semple ("just be simple"). The revised name, then, issues a commanding motto for Hughes's poetic program. And finally, "Semple" may also be an ironic appropriation of the middle name of Aimee Semple McPherson, the evangelist, who became a vicious and outspoken opponent of Hughes during the early forties.[11] It would be sweet revenge to name his irreverent, black-nationalist bard after a white evangelist who tried to censor and, failing that, publicly excoriated Hughes's poetry.

Simple's provocative name, his rich and original use of language, his obstinate literalism, his radical politics, and his eccentric appearance distinguish him as a poet figure and associate him with a long line of poetic simpletons—most important, with Shakespeare's fools. This is especially obvious in a story like "Cocktail Sip," where Boyd says Simple sounds like an Elizabethan poet, or "Midsummer Madness," in which Simple composes pithy proverbs. Like a Shakespearean fool, the Hughesian bard often encodes wisdom in nonsense.[12] Indeed, the cardinal point of the Simple stories is the wisdom of simplicity—a precept that, when applied to poetry, demands a daring aesthetic program.

Shakespeare in Harlem (1942), roughly contemporary with the Simple period, self-consciously engages in wooing Simple's muse. The volume is exemplary for two reasons: first, because it declares itself to be "A book of light verse," and second, because it has been largely overlooked by critics (the latter point undoubtedly due to the former). That is, its outspoken aesthetic recalcitrance has almost certainly doomed it to critical neglect. To read *Shakespeare in Harlem* we need an interpretive practice that accommodates these poems on their own terms, one that strives, as Simple would say, to "listen fluently."

From the prefatory note at the front of the book,

A book of light verse. Afro-Americana in the blues mood. Poems syncopated and variegated in the colors of Harlem, Beale Street, West Dallas, and Chicago's South Side.

Blues, ballads, and reels to be read aloud, crooned, shouted, recited, and sung. Some with gestures, some not—as you like. None with a far-away voice   (viii)

to "A Note on the Type" on the last page of the book,

The headings are set in Vogue Extra-Bold, a typeface designed in our time with the aim to express the utmost simplicity   (125)

Shakespeare in Harlem equates the poetic with the simple. It declares itself to contain merely "light verse," "Afro-*Americana*"—a collection of folk materials—rather than high art. Like much of Hughes's canon, this book will employ folk forms—"blues, ballads, and reels"—that common readers are already familiar with from the oral culture. Indeed, the poet encourages readers to make the poems their own: they should be "read aloud, crooned, shouted, recited, and sung." Further, they can be acted out, "Some with gestures, some not." The preface, then, casts readers in the role of performers who will interpret the poems "as [they] like." The allusion to *As You Like It* is the first oblique reference to the namesake of the book. Yet this Shakespeare, *in Harlem*, is near at hand, colloquial, folksy; he does not speak with the "far-away voice" of Elizabethan England or literary convention or classical poetry. Even his typeface expresses the "utmost simplicity."

But the appropriation of Shakespeare into simplicity in Harlem is not merely an adjustment undertaken for the audience, nor is it entirely a political maneuver. When Shakespeare goes to Harlem, he faces a crisis of language that is figured forth in extreme simplicity. The material and psychological conditions of Harlem as depicted here (elsewhere Hughes emphasizes its many positive aspects)—poverty, hunger, violence, lack of opportunity, unfathomable despair—render him almost speechless; it is only through the fool, conventionally a voice of simplicity amid overwhelming complexity, that the poet maintains expression. Like Virginia Woolf's imaginative "reconstruction" of the life of Julia Shakespeare in *A Room of One's Own*, in which she tries to imagine what would have been the fate of Shakespeare's sister (that is, of a talented female poet in the sixteenth century), Hughes is to some extent exploring what Shakespeare's fate would be were he an unemployed African American in twentieth-century Harlem.

Little wonder, then, that the title poem—in which we first hear how Shakespeare sounds in Harlem—is half nonsense:

>   Hey ninny neigh!
>   And a hey nonny noe!
>   Where, oh, where
>   Did my sweet mama go?
>
>   Hey ninny neigh
>   With a tra-la-la-la!
>   They say your sweet mama
>   Went home to her ma.   (111)

The poem's nonsense syllables, as might be expected, echo a song from *As You Like It* which two pages sing in honor of the fool's engagement:

>   It was a lover and his lass,
>   With a hey, and a ho, and a hey nonino,
>   That o'er the green cornfield did pass
>   In springtime, the only pretty ringtime,
>   When birds do sing, hey ding a ding, ding.
>   Sweet lovers love the spring.   (V.iii.15–20)

Shakespeare in Harlem reverses this song: love cannot be idealized through images of springtime and green fields. *As You Like It* itself ridicules romantic equations about love, nature, and the simple life, and the nonsense syllables in the pages' song suggest the fatuousness of those idealized formulations. In the Hughes poem, by contrast, the allusion to Shakespeare seems to marshal the linguistic resources of the fool. Here the nonsense, rather than echoing the mindless babble of the clichéd lyrics, disrupts the portentousness of the lines that communicate the loss of love. Indeed, the first two lines of nonsense in each quatrain seem almost to make possible the utterance of the final two lines that admit loss.

The structure of the stanzas, then, which move from nonsense to sense, suggests that the incantatory energy of the nonsense—deriving from rhymes, alliteration, exclamation marks, and most of all from the liberating effects of non-referential language—is necessary in order to accommodate the painful reality of the sense lines. The word "ninny" in Hughes's stanzas can thus be read simultaneously as a nonsense utterance and a direct address to the fool, "Hey, Ninny." In both cases the special capacities of foolishness are invoked. Similarly, the literal "no" that is released in the nonsensical "nonny noe" provides an aural negation of the otherwise ineluctable misfortune of the sense lines.

And though the poem sounds somewhat whimsical, lost love is not a comic subject in *Shakespeare in Harlem*. The "un-sonnet sequence" that opens the book (another revision of Shakespeare), "Seven Moments of Love," demonstrates what the rest of the book will reiterate: that to be abandoned by a lover is to be cast deeper into poverty. "Supper Time" moves from poverty as an image of loneliness to poverty as the literal result of being alone:

> I look in the kettle, the kettle is dry.
> Look in the bread box, nothing but a fly.
> Turn on the light and look real good!
> I would make a fire but there ain't no wood.
> Look at that water dripping in the sink.
> Listen at my heartbeats trying to think.
> Listen at my footprints walking on the floor.
> That place where your trunk was, ain't no trunk no more.
> Place where your clothes hung's empty and bare.
> Stay away if you want to, and see if I care!
> If I had a fire I'd make me some tea
> And set down and drink it, myself and me.
> Lawd! I got to find me a woman for the WPA—
> Cause if I don't they'll cut down my pay.   (4)

The un-sonnet sequence, indeed the entire book, treats love as a social rather than merely a private problem. Abandoned lovers are exposed to hunger and cold, to diminished wages and status. Details like the dry kettle, the empty breadbox, and the lack of firewood function simultaneously as metaphors for the speaker's isolation and as factual examples of the hardships he will face living on only one income.

The title poem begins a process of recontextualization of private life that the rest of the book develops. In "Shakespeare in Harlem" a speaker registers his loss of love in the first quatrain and another person answers him with the reports of still other people ("they say") in the second quatrain. The poem, in a section of the book called "Lenox Avenue," obviously invokes the voices of the people living along the street. A man arrives home, discovers his partner is gone, asks where she went, and is answered by a crowd of neighbors that she went home to her mother. The communal nature of the event is further registered in the appellation "sweet mama" and in the lover's retreat to her own "ma." This is clearly a family affair, not the isolated nuclear family of suburbia but the extended family of a population that is shifting from the rural south to the urban north. (The Harlem resident's responsibility to aid even remote family members who move north is a repeated theme of the Simple stories.) Romance in this context is not the usual stuff of sonnets but a relationship modeled on the family, as the similarity between the terms "sweet mama" and "ma" indicates. The speaker's "sweet mama" has not left for independence or romance but has retreated to another community, where she will receive care: to her family. There can be little doubt that she is shrinking from the kind of hardships that the "Supper Time" speaker faces.

The poem's simplicity, then, has a great deal of work to do. The nonsense lines allude to a tradition of empty love sentiments even as they also tap the special verbal resources of the fool. The plurality of voices situates love as a public issue. The appellations "sweet mama" and "ma" suggest a paradigm of need and dependence that love can support but not conquer. Though the speaker may to some extent employ nonsense in an effort at "laughing to keep from crying," this cannot wholly account for the poem. After all, this is Shakespeare, a master of the oxymoron and paradox; that he resorts to nonsense and repetition indicates that his relocation to Harlem has taken a heavy linguistic toll.

"Shakespeare in Harlem" probably has echoes of another fool's song. King Lear's Fool advises that nonsense is an appropriate response (it is the sign, in fact, of some vestige of sense) to the extreme emotional and physical hardships that Lear and the Fool experience on the stormy heath:

> He that has and a little tiny wit,
>> With a heigh-ho, the wind and the rain,
> Must make content with his fortunes fit,
>> For the rain it raineth every day.   (III.ii.74–77)

The logic of the Fool's song turns on the double use of "little tiny wit": it argues that he who has a shred of sense left will employ a bit of humor to accept his situation, no matter how horrible it seems. The association of the fool's perspective with wisdom is here and elsewhere abbreviated in the word "wit" that refers at once to humor, to knowledge, and, most important, to a quality that humor and knowledge combined may inspire: ingenuity. In *As You Like It* Rosalind tells Touchstone what is true for nearly all of Shakespeare's fools at one time or another, "Thou speak'st wiser than thou art ware of" (II.iv.55). Hughes's simpletons are blood brothers to Shakespeare's fools.

The wisdom and ingenuity of the Ninny become apparent when we contrast two of the poems in *Shakespeare in Harlem*. In "Kid Sleepy" the title character, like Melville's Bartleby the Scrivener, prefers not to participate in life. To all of the speaker's efforts at imaginatively resuscitating him, Kid Sleepy responds, "I don't care":

> Listen, Kid Sleepy,
> Don't you want to get up
> And go to work down-
> Town somewhere
> At six dollars a week
> For lunches and car fare?
>
> Kid Sleepy said,
> *I don't care.*   (24)

The prospect of working for a pittance, of earning just enough money to continue going to work, does not inspire Kid Sleepy. The speaker of "*If*-ing," on the other hand, is brimming with optimism and energy, though he has no more material resources than Kid Sleepy does. He has, instead verbal ones:

> If I had some small change
> I'd buy me a mule,
> Get on that mule and
> Ride like a fool.

If I had some greenbacks
I'd buy me a Packard,
Fill it up with gas and
Drive that baby backward.

If I had a million
I'd get me a plane
And everybody in America'd
Think I was insane.

But I ain't got a million,
Fact is, ain't got a dime—
So just by *if*-ing
I have a good time!   (32)

The difference between Kid Sleepy and this speaker is that the second speaker, as he proudly admits in stanza one, is a fool. He can acknowledge that he "ain't got a dime," but that "fact" is countered by another, more important, fact: he has had a good time.

Kid Sleepy, as his name indicates, has utterly succumbed to hardship, while the "*If*-ing" speaker has turned nonsense into a survival strategy. And notably that strategy is a linguistic game that finds new uses for even the most apparently unavailing words. The very contingency of the word "if" renders it susceptible to transformation. The fool Touchstone in *As You Like It* recognizes a similar indeterminacy in the word. Touchstone explains that quarrels can be resolved not by determining the truth or falsity of conflicting claims but by rejecting these inflexible categories:

> All these [quarrels] you may avoid but the Lie Direct, and you may avoid that too, with an If. I knew when seven justices could not take up a quarrel, but when the parties were met themselves, one of them thought but of an If: as, "If you said so, then I said so"; and they shook hands and swore brothers. Your If is the only peacemaker. Much virtue in If. (V.iv.96–103)

Hughes's speaker also has discovered the virtue in "if," and he exploits its contingency in order to imagine a better life.[13] Further, the speaker's word game employs rhyme, alliteration, metaphor, and rhetorical extravagance in order to conjure linguistic wealth. Kid Sleepy's response to poverty and unproductive work is more sensible than the second speaker's, but it is killing him. His name tells us he is on the brink of unconsciousness, he drowses in the harmful sun throughout the poem, and, most troubling, he has almost no language. His final utterance, the one that ends the poem and probably finishes off Kid Sleepy himself, lacks a subject and verb—lacks, that is, subjectivity and thus the capacity to act: "*Rather just / stay here*" (25). The "If-ing" speaker, by contrast, uses "I" nine times in his short poem and not only employs a range of action verbs but creates the most crucial one himself. Indeed "coining" the word "*if*-ing" is another way he amasses his imaginary fortune.

These two poems suggest that the simpleton's penchant for verbal play saves him because it makes linguistic production possible. When Shakespeare gets to Harlem, he is dumbstruck. Having recourse to the voice of the fool is how he continues to write poetry. What I have been calling his crisis of language is an important theme in these and other poems. It is also, however, a structural principle in the volume. The book consists of eight sections of poetry, four of which have generic designations that are anticipated in the preface: "Blues for Men," "Mammy Songs," "Ballads," and "Blues for Ladies." Two other titles emphasize locale rather than genre: "Death in Harlem" and "Lenox Avenue" (the street where Simple's hangout is located). All these sections answer to the interests of simplicity in their folk forms, common speakers, colloquial diction, everyday concerns, and uncomplicated ideas. Even more interesting are the first two sections: "Seven Moments of Love: An Un-Sonnet Sequence in Blues" and "Declarations" identify forms that are far simpler than ballads and blues: "moments," "declarations," a "statement," and one "little lyric." These new designations all emphasize brevity, bluntness, and simplicity, and they all take the thematics of simplicity to the structural level. As we will see, the poems themselves function like little elemental chunks of poetry that resist complication and elaboration. If we can find ways to read these atomic lyrics, we will have begun to achieve fluency in Hughes's poetry of simplicity.

I will conclude, then, by looking at several such poems in the "Declarations" section. The section title warns that these poems are not meditative or subtle in content, not figurative or lyrical in form. Instead, they are blurtings that make poetry out of the obvious or even the obtuse. "Hope," for example, reveals that the speaker's sense of possibility depends in an ironic way on her or his impoverished mental and linguistic resources:

> Sometimes when I'm lonely,
> Don't know why,
> Keep thinkin' I won't be lonely
> By and by.   (16)

It is precisely the speaker's not knowing that makes hope possible. To know more, to think this out more thoroughly, would surely mean the eradication of all hope. The speaker's language supports the sense that inarticulateness is bliss; the last line, "By and by," is a phrase from spirituals and hymns, songs that turn from misery toward hope by positing another time when suffering will be alleviated and even rewarded.

The speaker seems not to know where this formulation originates, but it is nevertheless part of her or his severely limited verbal repertoire. The exhaustion and vagueness of "by and by," ironically, make it efficacious. Two insubstantial words create hope by putting the concreteness of a harsh reality (now) into relation with the abstractness of a better future time (then); and in the process the phrase conjures up an in-between realm of relation even though it cannot visualize hope in more decisive terms. Further, "by" is a homonym for the "bye" in "goodbye" and lends a sense of finality that shuts down further thought and thus staves off despair. "Hope" is achieved, then, by dwelling in an intellectual and linguistic limbo, by waiting in some state that is neither "here" nor "there"—a provisional state characterized by verbal simplicity. "By and by" defers all the mental and linguistic processes that would inevitably lead to the negation of hope.

"Statement" announces its simplicity in its title. And, true to its name, it offers only this bare fact:

> Down on '33rd Street
> They cut you
> Every way they is.   (28)

The speaker making this statement has no time for pondering the by-and-by, subject as he is to the perils of the present moment. The knife-wielding, anonymous "they" are not just the perpetrators of street violence but also other evils—hunger, poverty, unemployment, disappointment—that produce physical violence (as the dialect "they" for "there" suggests). The ubiquitousness of "they" and "every way" demands the full attention of this speaker, who can only state or declare the bald truth about life on 133rd Street. The conditions of his existence prevent him from analyzing, lyricizing, or elaborating his plight. The reader, of course, can do these things; in fact, to listen fluently *is* to analyze these brief utterances and elaborate recognitions and insights that move beyond them. But "Statement" itself remains a hard fact and thus an obstinate form that articulates the exigencies of Harlem.

Finally, "Little Lyric" self-consciously demonstrates the way that poetry

will be altered when Shakespeare gets to Harlem: The poem's epigraph
insists parenthetically that this little lyric is *"Of Great Importance"*:

> I wish the rent
> Was heaven sent.   (21)

What is lost in reproducing the poem here is the way the tiny couplet is
engulfed by the rest of the page. The white space that ominously surrounds
it is as crucial to a reading of the poem as its two lines are. "Little Lyric" says
visually that the sigh of desire expressed in the poem has been nearly
extinguished by the vast emptiness around it. The visual hopelessness and
fragility of the poem on the page are translated into language in the poem
proper. Like "by and by," the idiomatic phrase "heaven sent" does not
express a real confidence in divinity to pay the rent miraculously but rather
employs the unavailing concept of heaven to figure forth dumb luck. Since
there is obviously no heaven (as the hardships and injustices of Harlem seem
to indicate), or at least no heaven that is willing to intervene, wishing "the
rent / Was heaven sent" is merely an ironic way to acknowledge that the rent
will not be paid. Again the brevity of the poem, the sufficiency of its perfect
rhymes, and the elemental simplicity of its point are features that defy
further elaboration within the poem.

The "Little Lyric" enacts the near loss of language. It reveals in an
extreme form what all the other poems in the volume suggest—that utter
simplicity is the only adequate response to a dislocated life in an urban ghetto
in a racist country. Simplicity, as we have seen, sometimes takes the form of
nonsense and foolishness and sometimes takes the form of brevity and
obviousness. Both manifestations of Hughes's aesthetics of simplicity forgo
the complexities of "great poetry" in order to express something that is "of
great importance." Such poems would rather do right than write right.

NOTES

1. Easily ninety per cent of the poems in Hughes's canon are of the sort that I am describing as simple.

2. Jemie, Hudson, and Miller, among others, have persuasively demonstrated the intricacies of Hughes's jazz structures in these two late books.

3. Reviews in which these epithets appear are collected in Mullen.

4. The stories are collected in five volumes, *The Best of Simple, Simple Speaks His Mind, Simple Stakes a Claim, Simple Takes a Wife*, and *Simple's Uncle Sam*. Additionally, Hughes takes Simple to the stage with *Simply Heavenly*, a comedy about Simple's marriage.

5. In "Who Is Simple?"—the foreword to *The Best of Simple*—Hughes concludes, "He is my ace-boy, Simple. I hope you like him, too" (viii).

6. For a chronicle of Hughes's disappointments during these years, see Rampersad, especially chapter 8 of the second volume "In Warm Manure: 1951 to 1953." Ellison characterized *The Big Sea* as a "chit-chat" book during an interview with Rampersad in 1983 (202).

7. Hughes wrote at least four explanations of Simple: "The Happy Journey of 'Simply Heavenly,'" "Simple and Me," "Who Is Simple?" and the "Character Notes" to *Simply Heavenly*.

8. In his Introduction Mullen surveys the scholarship on the Simple stories; all the works he cites discuss either their racial politics or their prose structures.

9. One might wonder how a character described as an "Everyman" or a "black separatist"—that is, as a stereotype—can break stereotypes. That is, how can black separatism resist stereotypes when it, *by definition*, carries racist stereotypes with it? This is a subtlety that would not interest Simple, who accepts the necessity of his own racism and rejects the idea that African Americans should "overcome" black nationalist stereotypes. As long as white racism prevails, he will resist it in kind. See "Color on the Brain" (*Stakes* 106–110) for one of many exchanges between Simple and Boyd about this issue.

10. In "Cocktail Sip," for example, Boyd's quotations of Elizabethan poetry are juxtaposed with Simple's rhyming prose: "Zarita is strictly a after-hours gal—great when the hour is late, the wine is fine, and mellow whiskey has made you frisky" (*Wife* 47).

11. Rampersad explains McPherson's antagonism to Hughes in chapter 14 of his second volume: "McPherson had a specific reason to harass Hughes. She was one of the allegedly fraudulent ministers of religion mentioned by name in his 'Goodbye Christ'" (390).

12. For discussions of the fool that emphasize the wisdom of his simplicity, see Welsford, Willeford, Weimann, and Goldsmith.

13. In his chapter on *Henry IV, Part I*, Holland makes a similar point, describing Falstaff's way of using "if" as a habit of speech that liberates him from the world of responsibilities and permits him to enter a "world of imaginings" (119).

WORKS CITED

Baldwin, James. "Sermon and Blues." Mullen 85–87.

Goldsmith, R. H. *Wise Fools in Shakespeare*. East Lansing: Michigan State UP, 1955.

Hollands, Norman N. *The Shakespearean Imagination: A Critical Introduction*. Bloomington: Indiana UP, 1964.

Hudson, Theodore R. "Technical Aspects of the Poetry of Langston Hughes." *Black World* (1973): 24–45.

Hughes, Langston. *The Best of Simple*. New York: Hill, 1961.

———. *The Big Sea: An Autobiography*. New York: Knopf, 1940.

———. *Five Plays by Langston Hughes*. Bloomington: Indiana UP, 1968.

———. "The Happy Journey of 'Simply Heavenly.'" *New York Herald-Tribune* 18 Aug. 1957, sec. 4: 1.

———. *The Langston Hughes Reader*. New York: Braziller, 1958.

———. "The Negro Artist and the Racial Mountain." *The Nation* CXXII (1926): 692–94.

———. "The Negro Speaks of Rivers." *The Norton Anthology of American Literature*. Ed. Nina Baym et al. 2nd ed. New York: Norton, 1985.

———. *Selected Poems of Langston Hughes*. New York: Vintage, 1974.

———. *Shakespeare in Harlem*. New York: Knopf, 1942.

———. "Simple and Me." *Phylon* 6 (1945): 349–52.

————. *Simple Speaks His Mind*. New York: Simon, 1950.

————. *Simple Stakes a Claim*. New York: Rinehart, 1953.

————. *Simple's Uncle Sam*. New York: Hill, 1965.

————. *Simple Takes a Wife*. New York: Simon, 1953.

————. *Simply Heavenly*. *Five Plays by Langston Hughes*. Bloomington: Indiana UP, 1968.

————. "Who Is Simple?" *The Best of Simple*. New York: Hill, 1961. vii–viii.

Jemie, Onwuchekwa. *Langston Hughes: An Introduction to the Poetry*. New York: Columbia UP, 1976.

Miller, R. Baxter. *The Art and Imagination of Langston Hughes*. Lexington: UP of Kentucky, 1989.

Mullen, Edward J. *Critical Essays on Langston Hughes*. Boston: Hall, 1986.

Rampersad, Arnold. *The Life of Langston Hughes, Volume II: 1941–1967*. New York: Oxford UP, 1988.

Redding, Saunders. "Old Form, Old Rhythms, New Words." Mullen 73–74.

Welsford, Enid. *The Fool: His Social and Literary History*. London: Faber, 1935.

Wiemann, Robert. *Shakespeare and the Popular Tradition in the Theater: Studies in the Social Dimension of Dramatic Form and Function*. Baltimore: Johns Hopkins UP, 1978.

Willeford, William. *The Fool and His Scepter: A Study in Clowns, Jesters, and Their Audiences*. Evanston: Northwestern UP, 1969.

Chronology

1902   James Mercer Langston Hughes is born on February 1 in Joplin, Missouri.

1915   Moves to Lincoln, Illinois, to live with his mother and stepfather.

1916   Elected class poet for grammar school graduation.

1920   Graduates high school; spends summer in Mexico.

1921   Publishes first poem in *The Crisis* magazine; enters Columbia University, New York.

1923   Works on ship traveling to Africa.

1925   Wins first prize for poetry in *Opportunity* contest.

1926   Publishes first book of poetry, *The Weary Blues*; enters Lincoln University.

1929   Graduates from Lincoln University.

1930   *Not Without Laughter* is published.

1932   Travels to U.S.S.R.

1934   *The Ways of White Folks* is published; father dies.

1935   First play, *Mulatto*, opens on Broadway.

1937   Travels to Spain as war correspondent.

1938   Mother dies.

1940   *The Big Sea* is published.

1942 *Shakespeare in Harlem* is published.

1943 Begins *Chicago Defender* column.

1947 Teaches at Atlanta University.

1949 Teaches the Laboratory School, University of Chicago.

1950 *Simple Speaks His Mind* is published.

1951 *Montage of a Dream Deferred* is published.

1956 *I Wonder as I Wander* is published.

1959 *Selected Poems of Langston Hughes* is published.

1966 Journeys to Dakar, Senegal, to attend the first World Festival of Negro Arts.

1967 Dies after surgery of infection on May 22.

Works by Langston Hughes

NOVELS

Not Without Laughter. New York: Knopf, 1930.
The Big Sea. New York: Knopf, 1949.
Simple Speaks His Mind. New York: Simon and Schuster, 1950.
Simple Takes a Wife. New York: Simon and Schuster, 1953.
I Wonder As I Wander. New York: Rinehart, 1956.
Simple Stakes a Claim. New York: Rinehart, 1957.
Tambourines to Glory. New York: John Day, 1959.
The Best of Simple. New York: Hill and Wang: 1961.
Simple's Uncle Sam. New York: Hill and Wang, 1965.

PLAYS

Five Plays by Langston Hughes (included are Mulatto, Soul Gone Home, Little Ham, Simply Heavenly, and Tambourines to Glory). Edited by Webster Smalley. Bloomington: Indiana University Press, 1963.

HISTORY

A Pictorial History of the Negro in America. Coauthor Milton Meltzer. New York: Crown, 1956.

Fight for Freedom: The Story of the NAACP. New York: Berkeley, 1962.
Black Magic: A Pictorial History of the Negro in America Entertainment. Coauthor Milton Meltzer. Englewood Cliffs, N.J.: Prentice-Hall, 1967.

CHILDREN'S BOOKS

The First Book of Negroes. New York: Franklin Watts, 1952.
Famous American Negroes. New York: Dodd, Mead, 1954.
The First Book of Rhythms. New York: Franklin Watts, 1954.
Famous Negro Music Makers. New York: Dodd, Mead, 1955.
The First Book of Jazz. New York: Franklin Watts. 1955.
The First Book of the West Indies. New York: Franklin Watts, 1956.
Famous Negro Heroes of America. New York: Dodd, Mead, 1958.
The First Book of Africa. New York: Franklin Watts, 1960.

POEMS

The Weary Blues. New York: Knopf, 1926.
Fine Clothes to the Jew. New York: Knopf, 1927.
Dear Lovely Death. Amenia, New York: Troutbeck Press, 1931.
The Dream Keeper. New York: Knopf, 1932.
Shakespeare in Harlem. New York: Knopf, 1942.
Fields of Wonder. New York: Knopf, 1947.
One-Way Ticket. New York: Knopf, 1949.
Montage of a Dream Deferred. New York: Holt, 1951.
Selected Poems of Langston Hughes. New York: Knopf, 1959.
Ask Your Mama. New York: Knopf, 1961.
The Panther and the Lash: New York: Knopf, 1967.

SHORT STORY COLLECTIONS

The Ways of White Folks. New York: Knopf, 1934.
Laughing to Keep from Crying. New York: Holt, 1952.
Something in Common and Other Stories. New York: Hill and Wang, 1963.

OTHER

The Sweet Flypaper of Life. Text by Hughes, photography by Roy DeCarava. New York: Simon and Schuster, 1955.

ANTHOLOGIES EDITED BY HUGHES

The Poetry of the Negro 1746-1949. Coeditor Arna Bontemps. Garden City, N.Y.: Doubleday, 1949.
The Langston Hughes Reader. New York: Braziller, 1958.
The Book of Negro Folklore. Coeditor Arna Bontemps. New York: Dodd, Mead, 1958.
An African Treasury. New York: Crown, 1960.
Poems from Black Africa. Bloomington: Indiana University Press, 1963.
New Negro Poets: U.S.A. Bloomington: Indiana University Press, 1964.
The Book of Negro Humor. New York: Dodd, Mead, 1966.
The Best Short Stories by Negro Writers. Boston: Little Brown, 1967.

Works about Langston Hughes

Barksdale, Richard K. *Langston Hughes: The Poet and His Critics*. Chicago: American Library Association, 1977.

Berry, Faith. *Langston Hughes: Before and Beyond Harlem*. Westport, Conn.: Lawrence Hill, 1983.

Blake, Susan L. "Old John in Harlem: The Urban Folktales of Langston Hughes." *Black American Literature Forum* 14: 3 (Fall 1980).

Bloom, Harold, ed. *Langston Hughes*. New York: Chelsea House, 1989.

Chinitz, David. "Literacy and Authenticity: The Blues Poems of Langston Hughes." *Callaloo* 19:1 (Winter 1996): 177-94.

Cobb, Martha K. "Concepts of Blackness in the Poetry of Nicholás Guillén, Jacques Roumain, and Langston Hughes." *CLA Journal* 18 (1975): 262-72.

Cullen, Countee. "Poet on Poet." *Opportunity* 4 (March 1926): 73.

Dace, Tish, ed. *Langston Hughes: The Contemporary Reviews*. Cambridge: Cambridge University Press, 1997.

Davis, Arthur P. *From the Dark Tower: Afro-American Writers from 1900-1960*. Washington, D. C.: Howard University Press, 1974.

———. "The Harlem of Langston Hughes' Poetry." *Phylon* 13 (Winter 1952): 276-83.

Eggers, Paul. "An(other) Way to Mean: A Lacanian Reading of Langston Hughes's *Montage of a Dream Deferred*." *Studies in the Humanities* 27:1 (June 2000): 20-33.

Emanuel, James A. *Langston Hughes*. New York: Twayne, 1967.

Ford, Karen Jackson. "Do Right to Write Right: Langston Hughes's Aesthetics of Simplicity." *Twentieth Century Literature* 38:4 (Winter 1992): 436-57.

Gates, Henry Louis Jr., and K. A. Appiah, eds. *Langston Hughes: Critical Perspectives Past and Present*. New York: Amistad, 1993.

Graham, Maryemma. "The Practice of a Social Art." In *Langston Hughes: Critical Perspectives Past and Present*, ed. by Henry Louis Gates Jr. and K. A. Appiah. New York: Amistad, 1993.

Haskins, James S. *Always Movin' On: The Life of Langston Hughes*. Trenton, N.J.: Africa World Press, Inc., 1993.

Jarraway, David R. "Montage of an Otherness Deferred: Dreaming Subjectivity in Langston Hughes." *American Literature* 68:4 (December 1996): 819-38.

Jemie, Onwuchekwa. *Langston Hughes: An Introduction to the Poetry*. New York: Columbia University Press, 1976.

Kent, George E. "Hughes and the Afro-American Folk and Cultural Tradition." In *Langston Hughes*, ed. by Harold Bloom. New York: Chelsea House, 1989.

Mandelik, Peter, and Stanley Schatt. *A Concordance to the Poetry of Langston Hughes*. Detroit: Gale Research, 1975.

McLaren, Joseph. *Langston Hughes: Folk Dramatist in the Protest Tradition, 1921-1943*. Westport, Conn.: Greenwood Press, 1997.

Meltzer, Milton. *Langston Hughes: A Biography*. New York: Thomas Y. Crowell Company, 1968.

Miller, R. Baxter. *The Art and Imagination of Langston Hughes*. Lexington, Ky.: University Press of Kentucky, 1989.

Mullen, Edward J., ed. *Critical Essays on Langston Hughes*. Boston: G. K. Hall & Co., 1986.

O'Daniel, Therman B., ed. *Langston Hughes: Black Genius*. New York: Morrow, 1971.

Patterson, Anita. "Jazz, Realism, and the Modernist Lyric: The Poetry of Langston Hughes." *Modern Language Quarterly* 61:4 (December 2000): 651-82.

Rampersad, Arnold. *The Life of Langston Hughes*. 2 vols. New York: Oxford University Press, 1986-1988.

————. "The Origins of Poetry in Langston Hughes." In *Langston Hughes*, ed. by Harold Bloom. New York: Chelsea House, 1989.

Smith, Raymond. "Hughes: Evolution of the Poetic Persona." In *Langston Hughes*, ed. by Harold Bloom. New York: Chelsea House, 1989.

Sundquist, Eric J. "Who was Langston Hughes?" *Commentary*, December 1996.

Trotman, James C. *Langston Hughes: The Man, His Art, and His Continuing Influence*. New York, London: Garland Publishing, 1995.

Turner, Darwin T. "Hughes as Playwright." In *Langston Hughes*, ed. by Harold Bloom. New York: Chelsea House, 1989.

Walker, Alice. "Turning Into Love: Some Thoughts on Surviving and Meeting Langston Hughes." *Callaloo* 12 (Fall 1989): 663-66.

Contributors

HAROLD BLOOM is Sterling Professor of the Humanities at Yale University and Henry W. and Albert A. Berg Professor of English at the New York University Graduate School. He is the author of over 20 books, including *Shelly's Mythmaking* (1959), *The Visionary Company* (1961), *Blake's Apocalypse* (1963), *Yeats* (1970), *A Map of Misreading* (1975), *Kabbalah and Criticism* (1975), *Agon: Toward a Theory of Revisionism* (1982), *The American Religion* (1992), *The Western Canon* (1994), and *Omens of Millennium: The Gnosis of Angels, Dreams, and Resurrection* (1996). *The Anxiety of Influence* (1973) sets forth Professor Bloom's provocative theory of the literary relationships between the great writers and their predecessors. His most recent books include *Shakespeare: The Invention of the Human*, a 1998 National Book Award finalist, and *How to Read and Why*, which was published in 2000. In 1999, Professor Bloom received the prestigious American Academy of Arts and Letters Gold Medal for Criticism.

CINDY DYSON has written several books for Chelsea House and has been published in many national magazines. She lives in Montana where she reads poetry, hikes, and watches her two-year-old son, Simon, grow.

MATT LONGABUCCO is a PhD candidate in English at New York University. He teaches writing at NYU and Bard College.

RICHARD K. BARKSDALE is professor emeritus of English at the University of Illinois at Urbana. His books include *Langston Hughes* and *Praisesong of Survival: Lectures and Essays, 1957-89.*

ARNOLD RAMPERSAD is the Sara Hart Kimball Professor in the Humanities at Stanford University. His books include *The Art and Imagination of W. E. B. Du Bois*, the definitive biography *The Life of Langston Hughes*, and *Jackie Robinson: A Biography*. He is the editor of *The Collected Poems of Langston Hughes* and other volumes.

KAREN JACKSON FORD is assistant professor of English at the University of Oregon. She is the author of *Gender and the Poetics of Excess: Moments of Brocade*; forthcoming works include studies of Jean Toomer and African-American poetry.

Index